San Antonio, TX

SECURING BUSINESS INTELLIGENCE

Knowledge and Cybersecurity in the Post-9/11 World

Peter R. Ramsaroop, MBA, and Bill W. Oldham, MBA

EVOLVENT Press

Copyright © 2004 by Peter R. Ramsaroop, MBA, and Bill W. Oldham, MBA
"Securing Business Intelligence:
Knowledge and Cybersecurity in the Post-9/11 World"

All rights reserved. No part of this book may be reproduced (except for inclusion in reviews), disseminated or utilized in any form or by any means, electronic or mechanical, including photocopying, recording, or in any information storage and retrieval system, or the Internet/World Wide Web without written permission from the author or publisher.

For further information, contact the author at:

EVOLVENT Press
5111 Leesburg Pike
Skyline 5, Suite 506
Falls Church, VA 22041
703-379-2146
press@evolvent.com

Printed in Canada

Peter R. Ramsaroop, MBA, and Bill W. Oldham, MBA
"Securing Business Intelligence:
Knowledge and Cybersecurity in the Post-9/11 World"

Cover Design by Alison Ruh

1. Author   2. Title   3. Business
Library of Congress Control Number: 2003116449
ISBN: 0-9728247-1-5

Dedicated to the Associates of EVOLVENT who, on a daily basis, are facing up to the challenge of corporate security for our major public and private sector clients in securing business intelligence.

ACKNOWLEDGEMENTS

We thank our colleagues and major contributors to this edition: Robert Pinto, EVOLVENT's Chief Knowledge Architect, Paul Ramsaroop, Chief Technology Officer, Guy Sherburne, Senior Director of Federal Cyber-security and Dennis Buxton, Senior Director, Cyber Security Consulting. Their biographies can be found at page 219

We would also like to thank Karyn Kortan and Kathy Cardoni of iMRG Inc. for their assistance.

As always, our thanks go out to our families for their support of our efforts.

TABLE OF CONTENTS

INTRODUCTION
Understanding the Threat. 1

PART ONE

INTEGRATED SECURITY:
A NEW WAY OF THINKING

CHAPTER ONE
No Knowledge, No Security 7

CHAPTER TWO
Perspectives on Security. 18

CHAPTER THREE
Building Security into the Culture 54

CHAPTER FOUR
Knowledge and Security 65

PART TWO

KNOWLEDGE SYSTEMS AND
SECURING BUSINESS INTELLIGENCE

CHAPTER FIVE
Knowledge as an Asset 91

CHAPTER SIX
Dynamics of KM: Knowledge Junctions 108

CHAPTER SEVEN
Optimal Accessibility 119

CHAPTER EIGHT
Protecting the Human Capital 130

PART THREE
CASE STUDIES

CHAPTER NINE
Leaders in Knowledge Management 137

CHAPTER TEN
Cyber-security Initiatives in the Federal Sector 153

CHAPTER ELEVEN
Understanding the Cost Drivers 162

PART FOUR
LESSONS LEARNED

CHAPTER TWELVE
Global Alert Network 176

AFTERWORD 187

APPENDIX A—HACKERS 190

APPENDIX B—STATISTICS 199

BIBLIOGRAPHY 205

INDEX 225

SECURING BUSINESS INTELLIGENCE

Knowledge and Cybersecurity in the Post-9/11 World

INTRODUCTION

Understanding the Threat

America and the Western world are still suffering the aftershocks of September 11 2001. The events of that day undermined many of the assumptions that we made about our safety. The events alerted the world to a new kind of terrorism, one that can put companies out of business and claim countless lives. It became clear that terrorists could penetrate and subvert seemingly secure locations, destroying at will. In the wake of this disaster, Americans re-examined their vulnerabilities in all areas–among them the area of cyber-security.

The world of the Internet, networks and cyberspace had already been compromised numerous times. But until this point, the problem had been minimized by government officials and business leaders. Now, however, two facts are inescapable:

Cyber-crime is rampant. Cyber-crime can cause great damage to businesses, to the well-being of the American economy and to national security.

It became patent that a see-no-evil, *laissez-faire* policy was no longer tolerable, that the "network neighborhood" was not safe and that a new awareness was necessary.

Government and business leaders also grew more aware that our civilization is passing into a new phase. We are no longer in the age of industry, but in the age of knowledge. Whereas the principal assets of an organization used to be tangible, now our economy and national security rest upon secure knowledge. Furthermore, this knowledge is not confined to discrete written records hidden in private office files, but stored electronically in shared cyberspace where it can be misappropriated by unauthorized and hostile parties. Business leaders are more aware of these dangers, but few are doing enough to prepare.

Knowledge must be protected as an asset, and it must be protected as security, for the security of an organization and of the nation depend upon its knowledge being inviolate.

Thus, we face a new challenge: how to secure knowledge against unauthorized entry while at the same time making that knowledge easily accessible to those who need it. The answer to this dilemma has been sought by many. This has resulted in a variety of paradigms and systems–but all of them share a common theme: the foundation of proper knowledge usage can no longer be left uncontrolled and unregulated. Every organization must have an integrated program of *knowledge management*. Knowledge management has two main foci:

It makes the knowledge within an organization as open to common usage as possible. This concept deals both with explicit and tacit knowledge. Explicit knowledge is traditional knowledge i.e., traditional ways in which an entity's knowledge has been stored, such as in reports, manuals and so forth. Tacit knowledge is the knowledge of experts that is often not communicated in a way that is meant to be stored e.g., it is shared orally, such as in meetings and conversations, or in ephemeral media such as email or message boards. Knowledge management deals with how to harvest and save that knowledge, and how to create an arena in which all users in an organization can access the resource of that knowledge and, as well, the resource of other people who have the knowledge. It does so by providing resources in the *technology domain* and introducing change in the *human capital domain*.

In the technology domain: knowledge management introduces software that makes it easy to share knowledge in a variety of ways: easy and powerful search tools, the conversion of various media (email, word processor, spreadsheet) to a common, interchangeable language, nodules where it is easy for people who share a common expertise or interest to connect with each other.

In the human capital domain: knowledge management introduces a new culture in which employees are encouraged to share, rather than hoard their knowledge.

Knowledge management makes the knowledge within an organization as secure as possible. Proper knowledge management protects an organization's knowledge bank from being accessed by unauthorized users. It does so by protecting the technology domain and the human capital domain.

The technology domain is that of the computer–its hardware and software. This is protected through technical means: anti-virus programs, firewalls, encryption and so forth. But no system can rely upon technological tools to remain secure. Therefore, knowledge management must also address the area of

The human capital domain: workers must be made aware of the dangers of unauthorized access to knowledge and must be educated and acculturated to a new way of acting and thinking. Knowledge security must become second nature, as much as locking one's car door and setting the house alarm.

This book is divided into two main parts. The first half of the book discusses the security aspect of knowledge and knowledge management: how to protect against hostile misuse of knowledge, particularly, knowledge in cyberspace. The second half of the book focuses on the access aspect of knowledge: how to make the knowledge of an institution easily usable and accessible. We then present a number of case studies, and conclude with the description of a proposed approach to national security based on the principles of knowledge management, a program called the Global Alert Network.

It is our hope that you, the reader, will take with you a new appreciation of the challenges that face us and of the resources we can call upon to not only meet those challenges but to take our enterprises to a new level. We cannot defer these issues merely because they are hard to quantify, but must consider the future cost of failing to act.

Peter R. Ramsaroop, MBA and Bill W. Oldham, MBA.
Washington DC, December 2003

PART ONE

INTEGRATED SECURITY:
A NEW WAY OF THINKING

CHAPTER ONE

NO KNOWLEDGE, NO SECURITY

Security Is a Multi-Dimensional, Complex Area

We still hold in our mind's eye the terrifying sights of September 11: passenger airplanes plowing into the walls of the Twin Towers, followed by their sudden and catastrophic collapse. That morning, our complacency was shattered by an existential crisis. Nothing would ever be the same again.

In response to this enormity, industry and government leaders radically re-assessed their assumptions about what constitutes adequate security measures and urgently proclaimed the need to secure networks, information, assets and people. A Department of Homeland Security was created, broad changes in regulations and security practices were instituted, and officials in all sectors urged the development of new security technologies.

In particular, September 11 brought government and business leaders the realization that key to our survival and success is securing government and business intelligence–that tighter network security, backup networks, increased security in knowledge management and the creation of disaster recovery architecture are absolute requirements in our brand new world.

However, are the steps that have been taken adequate or even relevant? And what can we do on our own? To gain clarity about what policies and procedures will enhance our security, we must first clarify what we are trying to secure and what can threaten that.

What Are We Trying to Secure?

As recently as ten years ago, some businesses relied on paper documents as their key means of storing data, but today, most businesses rely on electronic systems. Information technology drives the way our companies operate. In the last decades, information systems have expanded, until they link all social sectors. Commerce, government, education, entertainment, health have all been changed, usually bringing significant benefit to individuals, as well as to the financial, industrial business, academic and service sectors.

If you walk into an auto parts store, the salesperson will use a computer to access your account. He can see all of your transactions and will know your full name, address, phone number and perhaps email address. He can determine whether or not you have enough funds to stand behind your credit card or check payment. He can account for every item in the store, see its wholesale and retail prices, and where it is located. He can contact suppliers and see what parts they have, and how and when they can ship them. He can compare prices of various suppliers. And every time he makes a transaction, software programs will note the change in inventory, item sold, tax paid, how it was paid for, and how that contributes to the entire earnings of that day, week, month or quarter. He has more knowledge about the business at his fingertips than his employer would have had just a decade earlier.

But while the linkage of these information systems makes our lives more efficient and makes it possible to access information and effect change more easily, it also creates an increased risk of exposing sensitive knowledge. In order to provide benefit, electronic systems must gather information and classify data. That information can be misused by criminals, economic rivals and political spies. It can even find use as military information. Many confidential business operations can be breached with relative ease by a cyber-savvy criminal. Even an untrained teenager can acquire a few free and easily accessible software programs on the Internet that will make him a formidable threat to any business that lacks stringent cyber-protection.

To illustrate how cyber-reality has changed the concept of secrets, let us use the metaphor of Sherlock Holmes. A hundred years ago, when Sherlock Holmes wished to obtain the documents used to blackmail noble families, he and Watson had to enter the blackmailer's house in an attempt to purloin the documents, which were locked into a safe (and in the end had to flee over a garden wall). Today, Sherlock Holmes might succeed in obtaining and destroying the incriminating information from his private study on Baker Street. The incriminating letters would all be email transactions stored on the blackmailer's computer hard drive. Taking advantage of the fact that the blackmailer uses a DSL Internet service that is always online and therefore a stable target, Holmes could use a software program to slide through a security vulnerability in Internet Explorer to easily gain access to his computer and control it. At his leisure, Holmes could examine every document, destroying or altering documents at will. He might set up an invisible "backdoor" so that he could visit whenever he wanted, in order to monitor and control the blackmailer's activities.

On the other hand, this blackmailer might have set up firewalls and virus scans to keep out cyber-prowlers. Furthermore, he could save his incriminating evidence in encrypted files, keeping copies far from his home, stored electronically in Singapore or China.

And so the physical medium of information is today much less important than it was in the past. And the electronic medium, while convenient and powerful, is very vulnerable. Today, when network systems crash, billions of dollars in international exchanges can be lost in a few short hours. Information can be stolen and (such as credit card information) destroyed, or subtly altered. A hacker can compromise a business site and quietly make one small change. When visitors to the site go to the FAQ page, they are given information that casts a bad light on the business. Or when a visitor contacts a bank to get more information, a copy of his form (with his personal information) is sent to the hacker.

Information and telecommunication technologies allow information-dependent processes to gain in capacity, speed and quality. But those processes are dependent on the reliability and availability of the technical system and resources. As businesses grow more connected electronically, the process grows completely dependent upon the integrity and accuracy of the system.

It thus becomes increasingly important to secure systems so that they will be consistently available and reliable, and will produce information that is accurate and protected against illegitimate modification.

Knowledge, both tacit and explicit, is spread throughout an organization. With innovations in technology and their near-universal implementation, knowledge can be anywhere–onsite or offsite–with some locations more vulnerable to loss than others. A cyber-thief can track your every computer keystroke by parking a van outside your business with the requisite equipment. That information can be picked up from a television screen located within two yards of the computer you are using. If your computer has already been compromised, whoever is monitoring it can even turn its microphone and video camera on and off at will.

Another aspect of knowledge security is simply knowing the value of your proprietary knowledge. If you do not know the value of that knowledge, you can easily leave it out in the open and even give it away to whomever asks for it. For instance, the National Crime Information Center publishes a sensitive manual providing the instructions for accessing the FBI national crime database. A few years ago, a producer for a talk show on KFI radio in Los Angeles found that this secret document had been posted on-line by a government agency in Oregon and a law enforcement agency in Texas.

Because the loss or misuse of knowledge can be so devastating, business leaders must know where the knowledge in the company is stored, and how it is deployed and managed. Without understanding knowledge and what needs protection, there can be no security.

Therefore, the answer to the question, "What are we trying to secure?" is that we are trying to secure *knowledge*. In order to secure it we have to know what and whom we are securing it against. But even more primarily, we have to know what knowledge is valuable, where that knowledge is stored and where it is vulnerable.

Without knowing these things, we are in the position of a battle commander who does not know where his troops are, where the enemy is, where his troops are vulnerable and precisely what he is trying to protect.

What and Whom Are We Securing Our Knowledge Against?

The most visible enemies on our knowledge highways are cyber-terrorists. But are they really the most dangerous? Putting it another way, the most dangerous threat to the Verrazano Bridge is a terrorist attack. But when you cross the bridge, is that your greatest danger? You are at greater risk from other drivers, high winds, poor car maintenance and intoxication. Therefore, when you cross the Verrazano Bridge, you make sure that your car is in good working order and that you are alert and a defensive driver.

What if you are so concerned about a terror attack that you will only venture onto the bridge in an armored vehicle? The answer is that you will pour incredible resources into a project that cannot be guaranteed to protect you. Even if you do acquire this vehicle, it may be so clumsy that some of its onerous safety features might be disabled. And when you need to get the car serviced, you might take it to Al Qaeda Car Repair, all of whose mechanics are illegal aliens from countries that are against us.

This may sound ridiculous, but you are doing the equivalent if you concentrate all your resources on unlikely sources of damage and ignore the more plausible ones; if you make your system so unwieldy that users regularly bypass its security features (for instance, they use simple passwords or connect to a secure network from a home computer), and if you allow hostile people, such as disgruntled employees, access to your information.

And let us not forget simple physical threats to the integrity of our knowledge systems. In one instance, Internet traffic was interrupted when a farmer in New Jersey accidentally severed a line with his backhoe.

What dangers is your knowledge vulnerable to?

Natural disasters, such as earthquakes, hurricanes, tornadoes and typhoons, can cause tremendous damage to the physical and informational infrastructure of an organization and to overlapping systems.

Power outages can disrupt networks, as was illustrated in the summer of 2003, when a fire in an upstate New York power plant brought down electrical systems across the northeastern United States and Canada, leaving tens of millions of people without water and electricity. Power outages can pull down firewalls and leave confidential files open to view. Loss of power in a bank can leave exposed networks and give almost anyone access to account numbers and identities.

There are cyber-threats from without. Some of this activity may be directed specifically at your system. Other such activity may be caused by *script kiddies*, a kind of Internet trawling system in which cyber-criminals seek at random for systems with particular vulnerabilities. Experts in the field estimate that the chance that a business computer system has been probed and breached at least once, if not numerous times, is at least 90 percent. And that is not to mention the numerous viruses, Trojan horses and worms that can bring your entire system crashing to a halt.

There is the danger of cyber-terrorism, although how much of a true and immediate threat that constitutes is open to debate.

Solid evidence does exist linking terror organizations as well as rogue states with an interest in attacking others through Internet attacks. Chinese hackers have launched thousands–tens of thousands–of attempts to enter

Taiwan's security system. These are surely not all the result of teenage pranksters. And the Japanese Defense Agency delayed instituting a defense computer system after discovering that the system's software had been developed by members of the Aum Shinrikyu terrorist cult.

Nevertheless, there is considerable debate as to how real a threat cyber-terrorism is. Many in the security industry tend to think that terrorists get much quicker and easier results with the technologies that they are already familiar with, and are unlikely to invest greatly in cyber-attacks. On the other hand, the imaginative scope of evil is hard to grasp. Even in retrospect, the horrors inflicted by evil men are hard to fathom–how much more the horrors that they intend to inflict.

The bottom line is that whether the perpetrator is a political terrorist, a professional hacker or a teenager with an attitude, the threat to your system is real.

In addition, there are attacks and breaches from within, which account for 60 percent of misused computer knowledge.

No matter how secure your business may be, your company's knowledge can simply walk out the door. Whenever an employee leaves the office, his or her tacit knowledge is still intact–whether in his or her mind, laptop or briefcase. An insider must, by definition, be trusted to use the company network, for otherwise, he cannot do his job. Yet on the other hand, an insider has the capacity to cause tremendous harm. Every day, employees walk out of the organization with an intimate knowledge of that organization's security architecture. For instance, after Alan Giang Tran, a network administrator, was fired, he hacked into the computer system used by two private companies and destroyed whatever he could, changing passwords, wiping out the customer database, and shutting down the web site and online credit card processing system.

The woman in the cubicle next to yours may be burrowing her way into sensitive computer archives and retrieving, destroying or altering them. The nice young man in Human Resources may use his legitimate access to files to steal proprietary information and sell it to a competitor.

Such employees are made all the more dangerous because they generally do not have to constrain themselves in fear for their jobs. Employees no longer stay at one company for their entire career, as they did as little as thirty years ago. A member of today's peripatetic generation can gain the knowledge of a company and take it with him or her to a job with a competitor. Some employees have first transferred sensitive information to a rival company, and then quit and join that other company.

Even loyal and ethical employees can constitute a threat to your organization's integrity. In 2003, the employees of more than half of all American companies had email accounts on the company's network. Yet only 51 per cent of companies whose employees were online had any sort of email policy to prevent emails containing critical data from being sent outside the server and to prevent the server from being infected by viruses.

Lack of training, human error and disregard for procedures can all put your knowledge systems at risk. This can involve a simple error such as opening an attachment to email, leading to the infection of the entire system. Or it can take the form of susceptibility to a *social engineer* (a con man). For instance, an employee may get a phone call from a man claiming to be an officer of the corporations' security group. The so-called officer advises the employee to use a secure password, in the course of which he elicits the password from the employee. With this information, the *social engineer* is set to compromise the corporation's entire computer security.

Cyber-attacks can originate from anywhere in the world, and they take a wide variety of forms. To note but a few of the more spectacular (but not unusual) incidents:

- In 1998, at a time of heightened international tension, the military logistics, administrative and accounting systems of the United States military forces were penetrated by what appeared to be a major cyber-attack by a hostile nation. The source of the attack was traced to the United Arab Emirates. As it turned out, the attack had been launched by three teenage hackers from California and Israel, using software tools readily available on the Internet, who had concealed their involvement by routing their attacks through servers in different countries.
- In February, 2000, servers hosting several large commercial websites on the Internet were flooded with connection requests, which overwhelmed the networks and systems–a so-called "distributed denial of service" attack. The resultant slow-downs and service outages cost more than 1 billion US dollars in economic losses worldwide. The perpetrator was a young Canadian hacker.
- On May 4, 2000, a computer science student in the Philippines released the "I love you" virus. This virus swept the globe, infecting nearly 60 million computers and causing an estimated $13 billion in

damage. The student could not be charged because at the time the Philippines' criminal code did not explicitly outlaw such actions.

- In November, 2000, a cluster of simultaneous distributed denial of service attacks were directed at thirteen Internet root servers–the main computers that manage global Web traffic.

- On January 25, 2003, a self-propagating worm dubbed Slammer, Sapphire and SQL Hell infected thousands of systems and caused a widespread disruption of networks. This worm demonstrated the vulnerability of systems and the problem of neglecting to use available protective measures. The worm utilized a flaw in Microsoft's widely-used SQL database. Although a corrective patch had been made available, a large number of system administrators failed to update their systems.

- In the summer of 2003, a worm propelled itself through servers running the widespread (and hence readily hackable) Microsoft Windows. Thousands of personal computers as well as business, hospital and government systems crashed worldwide.

- There have been many cases in which a healthcare organization employee, motivated by personal grievance, stole electronic patient records from unsecured systems and published them on the Internet.

- At the end of 2002, an employee of a major United States credit rating agency stole identification data from thousands of citizens with the objective of selling them to a gang of criminals involved in the growing area of "identity theft," used to defraud credit card companies and retail businesses.

- In August of 2003, a massive power outage crippled cities across the United States and Canada, including New York, Detroit, Cleveland and Toronto. Entire systems were shut down, leaving data either out in the open or erased from company files. Unauthorized individuals, either by accident or with malicious intent, may very well have gathered massive amounts of critical knowledge from these unsecured systems.

Key Definitions

Data. The reality that a computer records, stores and processes-generally raw and unadorned.

Information. What a person can and needs to understand about reality. Information is data endowed with quality content, business context and meaning understood by the user.

Business Intelligence. Making information available to the user in order to enhance the decision-making process-data collection, analysis, synthesis to information and user availability that enhances business outcomes.

Knowledge. What a person or business uses to convert data to information-arguably, the source of competitive advantage.

How Good Are We at Knowledge Protection?

Clearly, whatever steps have been taken since 9/11 to secure computer systems and confidentiality have been inadequate. Internationally, nationally and in the private sector, little has been achieved in dealing with the problem of cyber-attacks. Computers are still highly vulnerable to external or internal attacks, and to physical damage.

But if we cannot guarantee total protection (no more than the best alarms and guards can guarantee that a bank will not be robbed), we can at least adapt a strategy that will protect us as much as is reasonably possible, and that, in the case of an attack, will allow our system to fail with the least amount of damage. At one airport, a hurried individual rushed from a metal detector, which he had just set-off, into the airport's subway system. This caused a shutdown of the entire security and boarding procedure. By the time this individual was caught, thousands of people had been delayed, planes had been delayed, and other airports had been affected as well. That is a case of a system failing poorly. The system could be designed in such a way that it fails with as little repercussions as possible: for instance, the airport subway comes to a halt. That too would be an imposition, but on far fewer passengers.

Who you are, what you do and what you own are threatened in ways that no one could have imagined just ten years ago. The security and privacy of information stored in systems and shared across networks and systems are vital to every individual.

From the large number of recorded security breakdowns, we can draw the following conclusions about the cyber-dangers that we face:

- **Technical Resources.** The technical resources to carry out attacks are widely available.
- **Impact.** Due to the highly complex interdependence of global infrastructures, there is no good way to accurately assess the impact of cyber-attacks. Purely in terms of economic impact, some of these incidents have caused losses in the billions of dollars. Beyond that, a series of failures can be significant enough to have national security implications.
- **National Boundaries.** Cyberspace attacks do not respect national boundaries. In fact, perpetrators are likely to route their attacks through other countries in order to decrease the probability of detection or prosecution.

However, there are ways that we can protect ourselves, more successfully than has been the case so far.

- **Shared Responsibility.** The interconnectedness of global users suggests that the security of all depends on the responsibility of individual system administrators. Least secure countries or sites pose a security risk to all–a chain is only as strong as its weakest link. On the other hand, good systems security practices implemented by all make successful attacks more difficult.
- **International Cooperation.** The successful tracking and capture of perpetrators requires international cooperation on a significant scale. This cooperation is easier to achieve in controlling cyber-crime than in dealing with cyber-terrorism.
- **Constant Learning.** Organizations must understand the issues of securing information systems in an ever-evolving and increasingly complex environment. They must learn from past experience in order to ensure the continuity and growth of their security and information technology.

- **Public-Private Partnership.** Because most of the information infrastructure used by the public and private sectors is in the hands of the private sector, security cannot be a government-only responsibility.
- **Defense Against Common Patterns.** The tools and methods of attack, whether employed by hackers, criminals or terrorists, are similar to each other. Therefore, many of the technical methods used to combat such attacks are also similar to each other.

Cyber-threats exist all around us. We must understand the nature of these threats and take appropriate steps in the same way that a physician treats a disease: assess the problem, diagnose it, provide intervention, evaluate it, and finally reassess it to observe for new or recurring problems.

In the following chapters, we will learn how to take the proper steps to maintain cyber-security and how to recover from a breach as quickly and with as little damage as possible.

CHAPTER TWO

PERSPECTIVES ON SECURITY

Facing the Challenge of Corporate Security

You know that you must apply security to every level of your organization. Your physical plant must be secure and your workers must be reliable. Most of all, your electronic information must be secure. But what you might not realize is how susceptible to compromise electronic information is.

There are a very limited number of ways to break into a vault, but the variety of ways to suborn a bank are limited only by the imagination. The criminals of today are imaginative, and they share their ideas freely, crossing borders at Internet speed.

Your organization is akin to a bank, not to a vault. But let us take the analogy a step further. Imagine an old-fashioned vault: a massive, cast-iron box with a variety of key and combination locks, that can only be opened at certain times and by two bank officials, each of which is allowed only one key or safe combination. Armed guards at the safe's entrance only allow in bank officials whom they recognize personally and who present multiple proofs of identity. But as times change, the need for the money and documents contained in the safe becomes more immediate and frequent. The process of accessing the safe is too cumbersome–the bank is keeping its assets safe, but its performance is inferior to that of its competitors.

The challenge that the bank faces is how to make the contents of the vault more easily accessible, yet at the same time as secure as they have been. If bank officials do not understand who the new thieves are and how they operate, they are almost certain to compromise the security of their vault contents.

Your business is the same. You cannot keep your records confined to metal filing cabinets. They must be on electronic systems–even though the minute they are, they are vulnerable to attack. Consider the following:

- In the year 2000, a teenage hacker, known as Coolio, broke into RSA–a cryptography company specializing in computer security.
- When customers entered personal information on the Intuit Web site–a site dedicated to monetary planning and financial security–a design flaw allowed the information to be passed on to DoubleClick, an advertising company.
- Every year, thousands of flaws in basic software are discovered –each one of which can be taken advantage of by a hostile attacker.
- Among other websites that have been defaced by hackers are the United States Justice Department, the Parliament of India, the Association for Windows NT System Professionals; as well as hundreds more.

And consider this as well:

- In 1978, Stanley Marvin Rifkin took advantage of Security Pacific National Bank's electronic systems to pirate ten million, two hundred thousand dollars to his own bank account.

Had Rifkin not bragged of his exploit (to his lawyer), he might have remained unsuspected. What makes this case different from the previous ones is that Rifkin made use of no technical computer knowledge to execute his bank heist–the largest in history. What he did took about thirty minutes, and he did it solely by speaking on the phone to a handful of bank employees. No bandanna, no shotgun, no knowledge of computer code and no Mission Impossible technical brilliance were needed.

If our systems are so porous, how can we protect them at all? The answer is that we must learn exactly where the system is porous. We must plug up software holes and educate our workers so that they do not unwittingly provide covert entrance to attackers. We must estimate our liabilities, the likelihood of attack and the damage that can be caused, the cost of security, and unintended side-effects of the security measures that we undertake. (For an instance of the latter, if you own two cars and you buy a car alarm for the more expensive one, you have now made it more likely for the other car to be stolen.)

If someone is truly dedicated to penetrating our system, he will, sooner or later, succeed to a greater or lesser extent. We must work out worst-case scenarios in order to assure that we fail with as little damage as possible.

Despite our tendency to solve our problems with technology, we cannot rely upon technology to provide security. Technology is only one of the components. No matter how much a machine can do, it works best when augmenting human alertness, not as a substitute for that alertness.

By way of illustration, on December 14, 1999, Benni Antoine Noris took a ferryboat from Victoria Island, British Columbia, to Washington state. When the ferryboat arrived at customs in Port Angeles, everything about him checked out except for the fact that he was "hinky." This was the term that customs agent Diana Dean used to describe his behavior. Noris seemed nervous–he was sweating, fidgety and avoided eye contact. When Noris's car was searched, customs officials discovered that a suitcase bomb lay in the trunk of the car. Benni Antoine Noris was actually Ahmed Ressam, who had planned to take the suitcase to the Los Angeles International Airport, put it on a luggage case and leave it there to explode.

A computer may be able to check a million names or compare a million fingerprints. But every computer security system can be compromised. Will a criminal or terrorist have to go through a fingerprint checking monitor? He can pick up the impression of someone else's fingerprint. Will a computer compare his iris to its databank? He can take a photo of someone else's eye, cut out a hole for the pupil and hold it in front of his own eye. He is much less likely to succeed if he tries to do such things under the gaze of a trained guard. And even if he possesses the necessary I.D., he is much less likely to succeed if a guard identifies his behavior as being "hinky."

Flatland

Security depends on looking at all aspects of your organization, and understanding how these aspects intertwine and work as a complex system.

Your system's vulnerability, its porousness, lies primarily where information is being shared. This implicates your organization's relationship with the Internet. It should be clear that buying a virus scanner and a firewall is not enough to acquire security. Besides the issue of human fallibility, such devices are insufficient for the simple reason that the Internet is a constantly changing entity. Capabilities change, criminal's knowledge and abilities change, exploitable flaws come to light–in short, a rock-solid system of 2003 may be a wormhole-riddled system of 2004. Security is a process, not a static system. Security is ongoing and develops to fit the contours of present threats.

In addition to Internet access, your organization most likely makes use of an "intranet"–a private system limited to members of your organization. This system too can be penetrated at many points, whether by people within or outside of the organization. Here, as well, no great know-how is necessarily required. A well-dressed executive from another branch of the company is anxiously waiting to meet someone in the waiting room. His plight has caught the attention of the receptionist, and when he asks her if he can go into one of the conference rooms so that he can plug in his laptop and do some work, she obligingly agrees. The executive thanks her, finds the conference room and a half hour later thanks her again on the way out. But he is not an executive from another branch. By getting on the Ethernet in a conference room, he has bypassed the security system that the organization uses to block outsiders from access to its system. During his few minutes in the conference room, he set up a backdoor that will give him instant, invisible access to the organization's intranet system at his leisure. Clearly, any employee can make equally devastating use of confidential organizational information.

As little as four years ago, few small businesses and personal users utilized the Web. By 2003, there was a 50% increase of Internet users in businesses of all sizes (American Management Association). Nowadays, by contrast, anyone can within a half hour set up his or her own web site.

There is only one commodity on your electronic systems, and that is information, and information contains vital and powerful knowledge. The effective use of information transferred over ten million dollars into Stanley Rifkin's bank account. The effective use of information has allowed a Gazprom employee to sabotage Russian oil and pipe lines by opening them via the computer systems.

The effective use of information has resulted in the appropriation of tens of thousands of credit card numbers. Therefore, securing a business is very much a function of securing that business's information.

To gain such business security, we must look at the threats to that knowledge. In response, we must develop policies and strategies that will prevent its loss and, in the event of loss, assure its recovery.

The inhabitants of Edwin Abbott's classic, *Flatland,* occupy a two-dimensional universe. To a Flatland inhabitant, the ultimate security is an enclosed figure, such as a circle. Nothing can get through it. Imagine the shock of a Flatlander to discover that the gold that he hid in his impregnable fortress has inexplicably disappeared. Try as the Flatland police may to solve the problem, they are stymied. But the case is inexplicable only to a Flatlander. We understand that in a three-dimensional world, a circle is no barrier to intrusion. That Flatland fortress was the target of a simple three-dimensional incursion. Unfortunately for Flatlanders, such an event is beyond their imagination. Thus, they are unable to foresee and protect against such an attack.

Until we gain more information and expand our awareness of the dangers we face, we are in the position of those bewildered and naive Flatlanders. The world is bigger than Flatland, and we cannot afford to live in little Flatlands of our own limitations.

To protect our business knowledge, we must first expand our own knowledge and awareness.

THREATS TO INFORMATION TECHNOLOGY (illustrative examples)					
Actions of Individuals				**Emergencies and Disasters**	
INTENTIONAL		UNINTENTIONAL		NATURAL	MAN-MADE
INTERNAL	EXTERNAL	INTERNAL	EXTERNAL		
• Employee sabotage	• Criminal or unlawful activity • Terrorism	• Lack of training • Error • Laziness • Disregard for procedures	• Authorized outside user with lack of training	• Fire • Flood • Storm	• Power Outage • Electrical Damage • Dam Break

Can We Really Be Attacked?

Prior to the events of 9/11, most organizations would have guessed that they were safe from attack. They used nominal software or physical security measures and that served to give them peace of mind. But 9/11 sent a new and chilling message: organizations can be attacked anywhere, anytime and by anyone. Now businesses look beyond the conventional in order to attain true security. Since then, the proximity of the threat has only been made more palpable by on-going intellectual property loss, natural disasters and power outages.

At first, when organizations were skeptical about security issues, they were reluctant to spend money on security. But now that the potential consequences have been starkly delineated, that disbelief is fading fast. Of 1,000 IT managers surveyed, 40 percent stated that information security was their department's number one priority.

Businesses have begun to realize that it is essential to secure their business knowledge from attack, and that total security involves taking into account the entirety of their system. The International Data Corporation estimates "worldwide spending on security and business continuity to grow twice as fast as IT spending over the next several years, reaching more than $116 billion by 2007."

The need for security is seen across the vertical market. In July 2003, 27 major financial institutions stated that the privacy and security of their customer accounts was one of their top priorities. In healthcare, providers, insurance companies and organizations will be required to install rigorous security standards to protect medical records and health information.

The threat is real and the time to act is now.

A Taxonomy of Threat Assessment

Threats to information technology can come from individuals and from emergencies and disasters.

Actions of individuals can be either intentional or unintentional. An intentional threat would be criminal or unlawful activity, employee sabotage, terrorism, et al. An unintentional threat would be in the nature of lack of training, error, laziness or disregard for procedures.

Emergencies and disasters–such as fire, flood, storms, power outages, and so forth–can be either natural or man-made.

Maintaining the security of computer-related systems is called *cyber-security*. Of the threats posed by human beings, some are **internal**–coming from within the organization, and others are **external**–attacks directed from without. In addition, there exist **natural** and **environmental** threats. Let us take a brief look at common examples of these threats.

Internal Threats to Cyber-security

Unintentional errors. To err is human, to forgive irrelevant. Once an error has been made, the damage has been done. Unfortunately, employees, employers and outside consultants err on a regular basis. If it is not properly dealt with, the accidental disclosure of business information can be devastating.

Risk Factors. No one can predict when someone will make a mistake. Prevention depends upon training, personal responsibility and the limitation of access to sensitive information.

Intentional Harm for Personal Gain. Because an employee may have detailed knowledge of systems operations and their vulnerabilities (both physical and electronic), he or she can cause severe problems.

Risk Factors. It is difficult to predict who is likely to engage in such activity and when he or she will find the opportunity to do so.

Intentional Personal or Institutional Concealment. An employee might hide pertinent information for a variety of reasons, such as for personal gain.

Risk Factors. Opportunity and ability are unpredictable. However, the general threat of financial or operational misconduct is somewhat predictable.

Intentional Institutional Harm. An angry employee can damage a company's integrity.

Risk Factors. Grievances, labor unrest and cultural conflict can generate powerful emotions, which can be hard to detect and control.

Insecure Business Practices. Bad partner communications, sloppy practices, unwise emails and lack of stringent email policies put a company's knowledge at risk for theft or loss.

Risk Factors. Poor policies, lack of confidentiality agreement, poor personal responsibility, competitors, poor network control (firewalls, patches, etc.) can all compromise a system.

External Errors

Opportunity Hackers. Those who break into computer systems without authorization are especially troubling because their identity and purpose are unknown.

Risk Factors. Motivation is unpredictable, and the threat is constant. Hackers exist all over the world, and their only limitation is opportunity and ability.

Criminals. Any illegal activity that seeks to harm a business or institution.

Risk Factors. Opportunity, value and derivative value provide a strong incentive for criminal behavior, and that behavior is difficult to predict.

Malicious Code. Viruses, computer worms, Trojan horses and logic bombs can cause serious damage and disruption of applications and computer networks, and can be costly to remedy.

Risk Factors. Such codes spread very easily and quickly. Busy systems are especially easy targets. Such at attack is very unpredictable.

Terrorism. Cyber-terrorism is the newest and most dangerous enemy, taking advantage of organizations' dependence on information systems.

Risk Factors. Cyber-terrorism is unpredictable. It can happen any time, any place and anywhere.

Natural or Environmental

Power. Without power, systems go down and security measures go with them.

Risk Factors. There is great uncertainty of occurrence.

Natural Disasters. These can cause physical breakdowns in security of buildings, computers and security measures.

Risk Factors. These are somewhat predicable and preventable, but hard to recover from unless one is prepared.

Vulnerability Assessment

Analyzing your organization's vulnerability is crucial in securing its integrity. Your system's vulnerability is its weakest link, and can exist anywhere. Your system may be riddled with a profusion of vulnerabilities–all of them must be identified and dealt with.

Although cyber-threats are highly unpredictable, what is predictable is that they are highly likely to occur in some shape or another. In order to protect against the profusion and variety of such threats, you must be able to protect your stored knowledge and intelligence adequately. And that requires undertaking an intense system assessment and correction.

The problem of porousness will only get more acute. In the not-too-distant future, many common office items, such as copiers, fax machines and printers will be assigned Internet capabilities. The critical data stored in those machines will be susceptible to hostile attack.

Reaching clarity about where your vulnerabilities lie and what your risks are is called *risk assessment*, and it is a vital part of any organization's security program.

This is not a matter that can be relegated to a simple formula. First of all, some information about risk is not particularly accurate. How good are the statistics that you are using? Consider that many companies will not report instances of cyber-theft because they do not want to ruin their reputations for safety and reliability. On the other hand, security firms may exaggerate the risk of cyber-theft. Whom do you believe?

How do you apply the statistics to your own particular situation? Certain factors may make your situation different than the norm. The clarity you seek is elusive. Reality has fuzzy edges.

Risk Assessment

Consider the following causes of death.

Cancer
Deer (collisions with vehicles)
Diabetes
Dogs
Floods
Flu and pneumonia
Food poisoning

Heart disease
HIV
Hurricanes
Lightning
Motor vehicle accidents
Mountain lions
Murder
Nursery product accidents (cribs, cradles, etc.)
Plane accidents
Playground equipment accidents
Residential fire
Sharks
Snakes
Tornadoes
Train accidents
Upholstered furniture (catching on fire)

If you were the Surgeon General of the United States, what use would you make of this list? What if you were the president of a Fortune 500 company, the head of a daycare center, the CEO of a national chain of stores? The parent of a two-year-old about to go on a cross-country trip to visit Grandma?

Whatever your role, you would first want to know which events are more likely to occur. The answer to that question depends largely on your particular situation. Citizens of Nebraska can set aside concerns about dying in shark attacks, and hospice residents need not worry about playground equipment accidents.

Secondly, within your particular situation, you would want to know statistical evidence and not just rely on the impressions you have gained from reading news reports. What about that cross-country trip to Grandma? Should you drive or take an airplane? In the United States, fatal plane crashes kill about 600 people a year; fatal car crashes kill about 40,000 people. How about the danger posed by cribs, cradles, and so forth? Death by upholstered furniture catching on fire is about ten times more likely to occur.

What if you are a security officer at a corporation? There, your assessment of risk applies to different phenomena–to physical break-ins, cyber-security and the like. Here, too, you must rely on facts, not on intuition.

Thus, the first step to assessing your organization's situation is to undertake a vulnerability risk assessment. Such an assessment tests every aspect of your system, both as a discrete module and as part of the system as a whole. This assessment addresses security procedures, electronic controls, and physical controls. Unfortunately many companies, like individuals are blind to their own weaknesses. For this reason, Malcolm Collins, Nortel Networks president for global enterprise networks, says organizations should bring in third party specialist to perform risk assessment "in the same way you'd employ external auditors for company finances."

The assessment should address the capabilities and potential of cyber-threats. What threats exist? What damage can they do? How likely are they to occur? How much would it cost to protect against that damage? You cannot protect your system unequivocally from any possible damage. The most well-protected system in the world could not survive if it happened to be on the ground floor of the World Trade Center on 9/11.

After these factors are weighed, real-world decisions must be made. Shoplifting is an attack on a store's integrity and costs the store money. But posting guards may cost more than the shoplifting itself. Eliminating dressing rooms may eliminate most shoplifting in a clothes store, but that may cost so many sales that it is not worth it. The same principles apply to cyber-security. If a particular cyber-threat has only limited capability of causing damage and the defense against it has a very high price tag, then it may not be worth defending against.

A vulnerability risk assessment will examine a system's critical infrastructure and pinpoint its vulnerabilities. It will examine the physical, functional, operational, cyber, personnel and system environments. It will examine its internal and external dependencies. In brief, an ideal vulnerability assessment inspects every aspect of an organization, considering every piece of knowledge and characteristic of the company as an aspect of its assets. Then it provides realistic recommendations regarding defense and countermeasures.

When an organization carries out a vulnerability assessment and adopts its recommendations, it achieves the following:

- Protection of its system against compromise by hackers and other cyber-criminals.
- Reduction of the risk of future attacks and threats

- Savings of time and money that might otherwise have been spent on recovering from attack or disaster.

How Bad Could It Be and How Likely Is It to Occur?

Security in any system must be commensurate with the risks. However, the process of determining which security controls are appropriate and cost-effective is often complex and sometimes very subjective. A prime function of security risk analysis is to put this process onto a more objective basis. Risk assessment answers the following questions:

- What is at risk?
- What can go wrong?
- How bad could it be?
- How likely is it to occur?

The risk assessment that you carry out has to be realistic and rigorous—not subject to anyone's comfort level. And you must be prepared to accept what you learn, no matter how unsettling that might be. It is not enough to look where it is convenient to look.

And no matter how bad a situation your risk assessment discovers, your organization is not dying. It is not moribund and hopeless. Because your organization can recover, because it can grow more vigorous and strong, you must take the results of that risk assessment carefully and apply the proper measures.

Risk assessment will identify your system's weaknesses: the areas where knowledge from your network can be purloined or where it oozes into the public sphere. Undertaking a risk assessment is a crucial step in deterring attack, because it finds problem areas and corrects them before they can be threatened.

The risk assessment that you undertake is fundamentally a vulnerability assessment of your situation. Your vulnerability is your risk. You cannot control attackers but you can to some degree control how you deal with them.

Your organization may have invested millions of dollars in its technical and human capital. It must protect those resources. Doing so will not only keep the system running and its knowledge secure from threats, but it will keep customers and employees happy and project a positive and secure image, and that will in turn maintain or improve its competitive status.

Let us take a closer look at the details of risk assessment. Although there are a number of distinct approaches to risk analysis, they break down into two basic types: quantitative and qualitative.

Quantitative and Qualitative Risk Analysis

Quantitative risk analysis considers two fundamental elements: the probability of an event occurring and the cost, should it occur. The cost can be expressed in many forms. Simply multiplying potential loss caused by an event by the probability of that event results in an Annual Loss Expectancy (ALE) or Estimated Annual Cost (EAC).

ALE and EAC can provide a good starting point for an auditor in developing a quantitative risk model. Theoretically, you can rank events in order of their risk and make decisions based on that list. Unfortunately, however, the term "quantitative" is not as rock-solid as it sounds, and may lead to a false sense of confidence.

In quantitative analysis, your focus is concise and narrow. You are interested in precision and attaining clear and measurable results. You make statistical analysis and, using logistic and deductive reasoning, you report on specific events in themselves, not taking context into account.

Quantitative risk analysis can work well in some circumstances. If you use your car solely to drive to work, then it is relatively simple to figure out the cost of your car being in the shop (the amount of money you won't be able to earn), multiplied by the likelihood of that happening (the car manufacturer provides the figures). In the business world, quantitative risk analysis can prove useful to perform a classification based on well-defined factors–any instance where the variables are few and easy to track.

But in more complex circumstances, attaining such figures becomes slippery and hard-to grasp. What will it cost your company if your email doesn't work for a day? And how likely is such an event likely to happen? Can you come up with an expert answer to those questions? Probably not.

In these cases, the data are unreliable and inaccurate. At best, you can supply a broad estimate of probability, relying ultimately on a subjective viewpoint.

Take the risk of a cyber-intruder stealing information from your database. How likely is that to occur? Is it definitely likely, somewhat likely, somewhat unlikely or definitely unlikely?

Say that you have decided that this is somewhat likely. Now provide a brief description of why you have assigned this level of risk to that event. (This will be helpful when you review your analysis.)

Next, decide what effect this will have on the corporation. Would such an event be definitely high impact, somewhat high impact, somewhat low impact, or definitely low impact? Say that you decide that this would have a somewhat high impact.

Again, explain your decision. Repeat this process with every element of risk that you identify. Next, assign some number value for each of these levels. Let's assign the following numbers:

Likelihood		Impact	
Definitely likely:	10	Definitely high impact:	11
Somewhat likely:	8	Somewhat high impact:	9
Somewhat unlikely:	6	Somewhat low impact:	7
Definitely unlikely:	4	Definitely low impact:	5

To qualify the risk of an email breakdown, multiply 8 (somewhat likely) by 9 (somewhat high impact) to get 72.

What about the event that your company computers get infected by a malicious virus? Perhaps you decide that this is somewhat likely to occur and that it would have a definitely high impact. That's 8 times 11, or 88.

A fire burning down your building is definitely unlikely to occur, but if it did, the impact would be definitely high impact. That's 4 times 11, or 44.

An employee stealing your handbook of company policies is somewhat likely to occur, but would be of definitely low impact. That's 8 times 5, or 40.

Now you can make a simple list:

Email breakdown	72
Virus infection	88
Fire	44
Handbook theft	40

Your risk management plan will, therefore, put great stress on preventing virus infection, and treat handbook theft as trivial and possibly not even worth addressing.

Qualitative risk management relies on what may be termed a community body of knowledge–common knowledge–and incorporates actual experience. For instance, you may not be able to calculate the specific, quantitative cost of an email breakdown, but you can give a reasonable estimate of how that would affect the organization's functionality. Qualitative risk analysis is thus by far the most widely-used approach to information systems risk analysis.

Nevertheless, qualitative analysis will not automatically generate results. Used incorrectly–which is to say, relying on incorrect assessments of the facts–qualitative analysis can be riddled with internal inconsistencies and do no more than reflect the analyst's prejudices and lack of comprehension. A good analyst is an experienced and sensitive observer. He or she realizes that the analyst's tools must be modified to conform to every organization that he or she is involved with.

So let us assume that you have determined the threat–i.e., anything that can go wrong and change your system–be it a cyber-attack, fire or employee theft.

The next factors to consider are countermeasures to deal with your vulnerabilities. There are four kinds of countermeasures:

Deterrent controls reduce the likelihood of a deliberate attack.
Preventative controls protect vulnerabilities.
Corrective controls reduce the effect of an attack.
Detective controls discover attacks and trigger preventative or corrective controls.

When you limit your employees' access to sensitive computer systems, that's a **deterrent control**.

You put up a firewall and anti-virus program, and train employees not to indiscriminately open email attachments. That's a **preventative control**.

You immediately inform your employees when a virus is loose so that they will isolate their computers. That's a **corrective control**.

You set up a computer system that recognizes the presence of a virus, automatically works to protect the computer system and informs the relevant parties of a virus infection. That's a **detective control**.

Is all this correct? Of course, since information technology is the principal way that companies store, relay and use knowledge, your knowledge system is one of the most important items to assess for vulnerabilities. Those vulnerability assessments must be a pro-active process of discovery within your business.

The Enemy Within

A threat targets an asset. A threat can cause harm only when an asset is vulnerable and the threat exploits that vulnerability. Thus, to discover applicable threats, you must identify your assets and their vulnerabilities.

For instance, termites chew through wood. Your house is made of wood and you have termites in your basement. Thus, termites are an applicable threat.

Your neighbor also has a wooden house, but no termites in his basement. Therefore, in his case, termites are not an applicable threat. Nor do termites pose a threat to another neighbor who lives across the street, because she lives in a glass house. (Her house, however, is vulnerable to large and heavy projectiles, and, like all people who live in glass houses, she should not throw stones).

Clearly, your organization is a complex system with many assets and, correspondingly, many threats.

Areas of vulnerability are:

- environment
- power
- hardware
- software
- networks
- payload

The following table identifies classes of assets and their potential vulnerabilities.

	SYSTEM ASSETS AND VULNERABILITIES
Asset	**Potential Vulnerabilities**
1. Personnel	• Death or injury • Compromised integrity • Mistakes • Limited training • Accidents • Negative attitude
2. Facilities	• Lax physical security • Inadequate site • Inappropriate construction • Lack of contingency and continuity of operations plan
3. Network Hardware	• Susceptible physical configuration • Unprotected radiation and emanations • Vulnerable physical access controls • Vulnerable personnel controls • Vulnerable administrative controls • Poor security policy • Power failure • Physical damage • Equipment mean time to failure (MTF) • Lack of contingency and continuity of operations plan • Corrosion and materials fatigue or failure

4. Network Software and Files	• Vulnerable vendor passwords • Vulnerable trust files • Unchanged default configuration • Vulnerable guest log-in • Vulnerable plaintext passwords and privileges in tables • Susceptible interfaces • Inadequate protocols • Vulnerable logical access controls • Accessible root files and directories • Vulnerable trust symmetry (mutual trust between two hosts) • Vulnerable trust transivity (trust symmetry is exploited by a third party) • Session hijacking • "Spoofing"
5. Peripheral Devices	• Vulnerable location • Poor physical security • Power interruption • Inadequate local modifications • Poor personal security • Inadequate security policy • Poor local practices • Poor security training • Unauthorized connection • Phantom connection (network that is connected to another network through an unauthorized modem or other device)
6. Host Hardware	• Mean Time to Failure (MTF) • Inadequate power backup • Corrosive protection • Poor environmental controls • Corrosion facility weaknesses • Poor physical security • Poor configuration • Vulnerable logical access

7. Storage Devices	• Equipment failure • Residual data failure • Poor configuration • Vulnerable disposal of equipment, particularly of data storage devices
8. Host Operating System	• Vulnerable vendor passwords • Design flaws • Outdated security features • Poor protocols • Vulnerable languages • Compromised specifications • Unattended releases and updates • Poor configuration management
9. System Level Software	• Vulnerable vendor passwords • Unattended releases and updates • Poor configuration management
10. Application Level Software	• Unattended releases and updates • Vulnerable development environment • Porous access control
11. Operational Data	• Poor back-up and recovery • Poor contingency planning • Corruption, both deliberate and non-deliberate
12. Historical Data	• Media aging and degenerating • Poor recovery procedures • Vulnerable facility environment
13. System Security Features	• Insider system break-in • Deliberate attacks

14. System Security Files	• Insider corruption and modification, both intentional and unintentional
15. Power Supply and Distribution Systems	• Poor design • Corrosion • Power surge or current instability • Poor capacity planning
16. Environmental Systems	• Poor design • Poor capacity planning • Corrosion • Inadequate maintenance
17. Telecommunications Systems	• Tapping • Interception • Hacking • Physical disaster • Service interruption

Using these tables, at a glance, you have an overview of your company's assets and the kinds of threats that target those assets, seeking to destroy their value or exploit their potential. Putting together such an assessment is the single most effective action you can take to prevent attacks and secure your business. From the assessment flows everything else.

The only way that you can get where you want to go is to know where you want to go and how to get there. Without making an assessment, you might overlook crucial areas of concern and concentrate on relatively trivial matters.

Your vulnerability assessment will define, clarify, review and evaluate the capability and probability of the many threats to every aspect of your system. An assessment analyzes a facility, its environment and its functional, physical, operational, cyber, personnel and systems aspects. The assessment will take particular note of your organization's reliance upon computer technology.

The assessment must take the entire system into account and deal with all the factors that must be protected, including non-tangible factors.

An attack on an asset can have both obvious as well as more subtle consequences. For instance, in addition to all the other damage caused by an attack that erases critical data from your system, there is the issue of timeliness. Timeliness is vital to your organization's success, and such a cyber-attack, making it impossible for your organization to keep commitments or apply for new contracts, can be as devastating as any other damage.

Although your vulnerability assessment must deal with your entire organization, here we are focusing particularly on the cyber-aspect of your organization's vulnerabilities. There are a number of tools available to help you carry out a cyber-vulnerability assessment. These are:

- Network Mapping (using a port scanner)
- Vulnerability Testing (using a vulnerability scanner)
- Penetration (attack) Testing
- Security Testing and Evaluation
- Password Cracking Testing
- Log Review Testing
- File Integrity Checkers
- Virus Detectors
- Dialing Attack Testing

The following table lists these tests and points out their strengths and weaknesses.

VULNERABILITY TESTING		
Test	**Its Strengths**	**Its Weaknesses**
Network Mapping (using a port scanner)	• Fast. • Efficiently scans a large number of hosts. • Excellent freeware tools available. • Highly automated. • Low cost.	• Does not directly identify known vulnerabilities. • Generally used as a prelude to other testing. • Requires significant expertise to interpret results.
Vulnerability Testing (using a vulnerability scanner)	• Fairly fast. • Efficiently scans large number of hosts. • Some freeware tools available. • Highly automated. • Identifies known vulnerabilities from data base. • Often provides advice on mitigating vulnerabilities discovered. • Cost ranges from high (commercial scanners) to non-existent (freeware). • Easy to run on a regular basis.	• High false positive rate. • Generates large amount of network traffic. • Not stealthy–easily detected. • Can be dangerous in the hands of a novice. • Can miss the latest vulnerabilities. • Identifies only surface vulnerabilities.

Penetrating (attack) Testing	• Tests networks and hosts using methodologies that hackers use. • Verifies vulnerabilities. • Goes beyond surface vulnerabilities (showing how the interaction of surface vulnerabilities can be used to gain greater access). • Demonstrates real (not merely theoretical) vulnerabilities. • Provides the realism and evidence needed to address security issues. • Can test both the human and technical elements of security	• Requires great expertise. • Labor-intensive. • Slow. • Dangerous when done by inexperienced testers. • Certain tools may be banned by a host organization. • Expensive. • Can be disruptive. • Legal requirements must be met.
Security Testing and Evaluation	• Does not have to be invasive or risky. • Includes policies and procedures. • Generally requires little security expertise. • Addresses physical security.	• Does not verify vulnerabilities. • Generally does not identify newly-discovered vulnerabilities. • Labor-intensive. • Expensive.
Password Cracking Testing	• Provides clear demonstration of password strength or weakness. • Easily implemented. • Low cost.	• Potential for abuse. • Certain organizations restrict use. • Needs the full processing resources of a powerful computer.

Penetrating (attack) Testing	• Tests networks and hosts using methodologies that hackers use. • Verifies vulnerabilities. • Goes beyond surface vulnerabilities (showing how the interaction of surface vulnerabilities can be used to gain greater access) • Demonstrates real (not merely theoretical) vulnerabilities. • Provides the realism and evidence need to address security issues. • Can test both the human and technical elements of security.	• Requires great expertise. • Labor-intensive. • Slow. • Dangerous when done by inexperienced testers. • Certain tools may be banned by a host organization. • Expensive. • Can be disruptive. • Legal requirements must be met.
Security Testing and Evaluation	• Does not have to be invasive or risky. • Includes policies and procedures. • Generally requires little security expertise. • Addresses physical security.	• Does not verify vulnerabilities. • Generally does not identify newly-discovered vulnerabilities. • Labor-intensive. • Expensive.

Log Reviews	• Provides excellent information. • Only data source that provides historical information.	• Cumbersome to review. • Automated tools available are not perfect and filter out important information.
File Integrity Checkers	• Reliable method for determining if a host has been compromised. • Highly automated. • Low cost.	• Does not detect any compromise prior to installation. • Checksums must be updated whenever a change is made to the system.
Virus detectors	• Excellent at detecting and repairing viruses. • Low to medium cost.	• Required constant updates to be effective. • Server-based versions may have a significant impact on performance. • False positives issues. • Ability to react to new, quickly-replicated viruses is often limited.
Dialing Attack Testing	• Effective way to identify unauthorized modems.	• Legal and regulatory issues, especially if using public switched networks. • Slow

Edmund H. North has stated, "There's a difference between a gamble and a calculated risk." If someone walks into a casino and starts putting quarters into a slot machine, he is gambling. If you, however, have figured out the odds of winning, you may make a rational decision to take a calculated risk. You might tell yourself, "I have a one in five hundred chance of winning a hundred dollars every time I put a quarter into the slot. Those are not very good odds. On the other hand, I consider the loss of five dollars a trivial circumstance, and so I am prepared to risk that five dollars for the unlikely event of winning a hundred dollars."

In this case, your actions may initially be no different than those of the gambler, and so both you and he might get confused about the difference between gambling and taking a risk. But sooner or later your decisions will diverge from his. While he spends his money in the grip of a gambling fever, you will strategize and control your finances as well as you can. Whereas he will risk everything, you will as much as possible cover your losses–for instance, you may decide to risk only a certain amount of principal, and, assuming that you win some money, to risk only your winnings, not your principal.

In the same way, security actions taken by the managers of two companies, one of whom is reactive and the other of whom has made a risk assessment, may superficially appear similar. Both managers set up firewalls, urge employees to use strong passwords, and the like. But sooner or later their paths will diverge. The first manager will find himself overtaken by threats that he had not considered and dealt with, whereas the second manager will have set up a rational and robust security system.

Do not underestimate the importance of risk analysis. It will serve you well, for it is the foundation to your organization's entire security structure.

Securing the Frontier

Security is not a one-time event, like getting aluminum siding to protect your house from termites. Security is an on-going process that shifts and adapts together with the changes in your organization and with the changes in threats, as attackers grow more sophisticated and launch new and more powerful challenges to the integrity of your information systems.

The work of security, privacy and information assurance is best implemented by using a four-phase cycle:

- **Assess**
- **Address**
- **Test**
- **Monitor, Plan and Improve**

1. Assess

Assessment–a detailed evaluation of the organization's infrastructure to ensure an accurate understanding of its current security–has been discussed above. So let us proceed to the next element.

2. Address

Once you have identified weaknesses, you must put countermeasures in place to fortify your organization's security. We have already touched on this as well.

3. Test

The next step is to test your systems thoroughly. Verify that your security measures are doing what they are supposed to do.

Don't content yourself with having assessed the problem and assigned a solution. Test the solution to see if it really works. Do the software and hardware work as advertised? Can your employees follow the new procedures, or are those procedures unnecessarily difficult and obscure?

Make certain that your new policies work in the real world, not only in a procedures manual. It is strongly advised that you have an unbiased third party evaluate your new protective measures. Take care to properly design, implement and coordinate your systems, networks and policies, so that security will be a fundamental element in all of your products, services, systems and networks–so that security will, in fact, be an integral part of the system design.

4. Monitor, Plan and Improve

Even after you have ascertained that your system is working as planned, you must institute on-going supervision by experts who are authorized to continuously tailor processes and procedures to improve effectiveness and efficiency. But do not only rely on experts. Rather, involve all of the members of your organization. Invite their comments, criticism and suggestions. Have everyone engage in reviewing and reassessing the security of information systems and networks. Improve your defenses against present threats and maintain a flexible organizational culture, so that you can smoothly modify all aspects of security to deal with new and changing threats and vulnerabilities.

We live in a world of increasingly rapid change. Once the village elder's memories served as a repository of wisdom and information for the young, for that wisdom and information would serve them as well as it had served him. Today, however, change takes place so rapidly that this model has been overturned. We may mistrust those who were trained a decade ago or even a year ago, because conditions and knowledge are changing so rapidly, and no one can keep up with it all.

The application of that knowledge to how humans will behave must undergo constant revision. Therefore, constantly monitor, plan and improve. Your survival and success depend on it.

What Do You Have to Lose?

Once you have arrived at a clear risk assessment, you have to undertake a new series of assessments in order to determine what your risk management strategy will be.

Take the case of the family going to visit Grandma. Car travel is much more dangerous than an airplane ride. Nevertheless, it is much less expensive, more convenient, and you get to stop over to see some tourist attractions. You may decide that the risk of an accident is small enough to ignore. Another family may have a very different way of managing its risk: having once experienced a fatal car crash, the family will always prefer traveling by plane, no matter what the inconvenience and cost.

So when deciding on how to manage risk, you must ask yourself not only what the likelihood of an event taking place is but also what the possible damage is and how much you are willing to tolerate that for the sake of other factors. Let's say you are a mother in the suburbs who has just parked her car and needs to run into the house for a few moments. The baby is in the car seat sleeping. What do you do? You are an office manager who has come into the office on an early Sunday morning to email some urgent and highly-sensitive information. Unfortunately, you don't know how to encrypt a file, and no one is available to help you. What do you do?

In *Modern Times*, Charlie Chaplin plays a ne'er-do-well who gets a job as a shipbuilder. Needing a wedge of wood and finding one in a wooden framework, he knocks it out with his hammer. As a result, the ship, which had been kept in place by that framework, slides into the sea and disappears below the water. Charlie Chaplin performed a very poor risk assessment about knocking out that wedge.

But as for you, once you have identified threats, the two questions, "How bad is it and how likely is it to occur?," become of prime importance. Obviously, you cannot afford to overlook security risks and allow threats to damage your organization. Perhaps not as obvious, you cannot afford to spend your organization's resources securing against threats that are trivial.

Dr. P. G. Dory, former Head of Information Security at Barclays Bank, PLC, states that "we are rapidly approaching a situation where risk management is no longer an option. In a highly competitive business environment, companies cannot afford to have costly or inappropriate security. *Effective risk management can be nothing less than the defense of company profitability*" (emphasis added).

The following chart shows what a business stands to lose when its data bases are breached and its proprietary knowledge falls into unauthorized hands.

UNAUTHORIZED ACCESS TO THE COMPANY NETWORK	
Financial Significance	
Compromised Information and Network	**The Negative Consequence**
• Financial data used in the preparation of strategic planning, department budgets and financial statement documents.	• Material effect on financial statements.
• Trade secrets and proprietary information entrusted to public or regulatory agencies.	• Research and clinical trials.
• Theft of intellectual property.	• Loss of intellectual property.
• Provider, health groups, insurance plans, eligibility and coverage, contract, pharmaceutical, billing, reimbursement.	• Fraud and abuse.
• Use of system for sexual harassment, defamation and other illegal or proscribed purposes or actions.	• Criminal, civil and administrative findings.
• One party fails to secure its systems, which are consequently used to attack other systems, causing loss to third parties.	• Downstream liability.
• Denial that an event, action or agreement took place.	• Repudiation.

Indirect Value Significance	
• Personal or command information that would be of unusual interest to employees and others.	• Adverse effect on employee morale • Loss of productivity • Embarrassment to the management or employees. • Loss of reputation. • Impairment of mission.
Intelligence, Confidentiality and Privacy Significance	
• Private and sensitive information about an individual or entity.	• Disclosure or misuse of private information. • Regulatory, criminal and civil transgressions.
• Information protected by regulation or information that is a prime candidate for regulatory protection.	• Regulatory intervention.
• Disclosure of sensitive information of national value.	• Harm to society or to the government.

Risk Management

Once you have established what your vulnerabilities are, you must deal with the issues that put your organization at risk. This is called *risk management*.

Cyber-damage can cost an organization hundreds of millions of dollars in disruption to the organization and its customers. In a few short hours, a malicious computer virus can propagate itself across the world, causing billions of dollars of economic damage. Thus has the quickness and ease of the Internet brought its own Achilles heel.

It is crucial that an organization engage in aggressive and systematic risk management. That management must be a comprehensive undertaking that involves the integrated handling of four major risk categories:

- **Security risk.** Are systems and information secure?
- **Technical risk.** Does the system work?
- **Organizational risk.** Can the organization use the system?
- **Business risk.** Does the system produce the desired results?

Many organizations focus on technical issues alone, leaving security, organizational and business risks to chance. Today that does not suffice. An organization must assess and mitigate all four kinds of risks. Failure to do so constitutes a certain recipe for disruption and even disaster.

Managing Security Risks

Security risks and threats to a system's critical infrastructure must be assessed thoroughly and managed aggressively. The infrastructure consists of information, information technology systems and networks and physical facilities. Only such an assessment and management can assure that these infrastructures are not liable to damage or compromise. This aspect of maintenance is known as *information assurance* (other sections of this book will deal specifically with these issues).

Managing Technical Risks

Technical risk is associated with critical questions. Will the system work? Will it work on time? Will it come in on budget?

Usually, technical risk is handled by a combination of an organization's own information professionals and outsourced information professionals. There are three primary categories of mitigating technical risk:

- Developing a sound project that focuses on the delivery of the technical system.
- Rigorous project management to ensure that the technical delivery will be on time and on budget.
- The use of systematic procedures to keep users up-to-date. Organization members must understand the scope of the technical implementation so that they can adjust to the new system.

Managing Organizational Risks

Dutch Holland, CEO of Holland & Davis identifies organizational risk as the risk that an organization will not fully utilize a new system. Failure to use a new system can be caused by any number of factors, one of the most common of which is workforce resistance.

The primary approach to mitigate organizational risk is the systematic and comprehensive application of *change management*. Change management is the body of knowledge that is used to ensure that a complex change achieves the right results in the right time frame and at the right costs. Change management sees to it that members and sections of the organization accept a new system and will use it.

There are three primary categories in mitigating organizational risk:

- Rigorous project management that makes sure that organization members have adjusted their procedures to be in alignment with the new system about to be put in place.
- Comprehensive communication with all employees, discussing the objectives of the new system (including providing an answer to the question, "What's in it for me?"), and the vision for the organization as it uses the new system.
- A performance management system that will monitor the categories of job positions that are needed to implement the new system.

Managing Business Risks

Business risk refers to the possibility that the newly-implemented system will not pay for itself. Such a failure can be the result of any number of factors, one of the most common of which is a lack of alignment between imbedded processes and the organization's business objectives.

There are three primary categories of mitigating business risk:

- The system must have both the integrating efficiencies that the company needs as well as the imbedded processes that the company will be able to use in order to get results over the long term.
- Business process documentation must be maintained, so that as the organization implements the new system, it does so in a way that the workforce finds logical and easy to carry out.

- The organization must supply user training, which will allow users to operate the new system not only mechanically, but with understanding.

Contingency Planning

Everyone is familiar with the failure of France's Maginot Line, an impregnable barrier to German troops. The Germans merely entered France through Belgium, thus circumventing the problem altogether.

No matter how thoroughly we protect ourselves against danger, it can always arrive from an unexpected route. No matter how thoroughly we update and rethink our systems, our blind spot will always leave vulnerabilities that we fail to foresee. Therefore, it is imperative to develop a counteraction plan if and when a disaster strikes.

Such contingency plans must be integrated into the general process of securing a business. This is because the type of contingency plans made depends greatly on the results of a company's assessment of risk.

One contingency plan is called a Contingency of Operations Plan, or *COOP*. The COOP is the master document that is implemented when disaster strikes. It contains all of the information required to successfully and cost-effectively reconstitute operations, and it also addresses peripheral ingredients for success.

In the event of a disaster, the COOP is automatically put into effect. Disaster-preparedness technicians can be at hand as the COOP is implemented, as well as when follow-up actions need to be implemented and when the process needs to be reviewed.

Other contingency plans include tools and measures such as quick reaction teams, corporate policies, critical process/system identification, recall rosters, alternate operating locations, formalized partnering agreements, "fly-away" kits and management emphasis. When properly developed for an institution and fully understood by its employees and associates, these measures greatly increase its chance of surviving a disaster.

Leading contingency planning and continuity-of-operations corporations can provide tailored and specialized services. These services should include policy, instructions, and recommendations for all company personnel and their families. They should also provide specific checklists that cover critical processes and that address the steps needed to make sure that a transition to continued operations is timely and successful.

When a company has a contingency plan, it provides itself with a competitive advantage over companies whose systems are not fully secure or which lack a plan altogether. Because the existence of a contingency plan results in a highly-competitive company, employee turnover is likely to be diminished–which in turn bolsters the company's security.

Think About It

Thinking about the details of organizational security may inspire the anxiety that accompanies any investigation that might threaten one's complacency. For instance, no one in more-or-less good health wants to invest time in reading about the negative consequences of not exercising and eating healthful foods. If we do feel some physical distress, then we may wish to avoid the doctor altogether, because we are afraid of what he or she may find. And we do not want to read about diseases that we cannot do anything about, nor do we wish to become hypochondriacs obsessed with our health.

The answer to such fears is that knowledge is not a burden–knowledge is empowering. If you have a health problem, learning clearly what it is and what your options are can only help. And being a hypochondriac is not caused by knowledge–knowledge only makes one an educated hypochondriac.

The same holds for your knowledge about your organization. Find out what dangers exist, what dangers your organization is vulnerable to and what options you have to take. The more knowledgeable you are, the more intelligent and effective decisions you can make.

When you stand in the dark, you may be protected from the sight of dragons, but you also cannot take a step in any direction. It can be distressing to turn on the light–to know clearly and unambiguously the shortcomings and limitations of your situation. But on the other hand, you are empowered–first of all, because you can see the dragons that exist and see that many of the dragons that you feared do not exist. And once you look a dragon straight in the eye, you may find that it is not so frightening, not overwhelming at all. You may find yourself ready and eager to do battle with it.

Therefore, turn the light onto the confusion and darkness that may now be shrouding your organization's security and security activities. See where the dragons of the cyber-world–hackers, viruses, corrupt insiders, compromised firewalls–stand. Their danger is finite and channeled into certain patterns. Your job–to beat them back–may be a comprehensive one, but it is not an infinite one. Vague dangers resolve themselves and crystallize into specific challenges when you analyze your situation and apply to it the resources of knowledge and considered strategy.

To extend the metaphor, dragons are known for hoarding upon masses of stolen wealth. In the same way, the dragons that threaten your organization can rob your organization's wealth: its financial base, its knowledge base, and its customer base. But you can be your company's dragon-slayer.

The first step is to see where those dragons lie, what their attributes are, what assets you have and the most effective strategies that you can take. Taking an inventory of your organization and its place in the world (including its cyber-environment) is one of the most powerful steps you can take. It is the first step to security and superior performance.

Think about it: think about your organization's security, its weaknesses and strengths, the challenges it faces and the options it has. Assessing your risk and then managing your risk are the vital underpinnings to your organization's security and health.

CHAPTER THREE

BUILDING SECURITY INTO THE CULTURE

Develop a "Culture of Security"

Our world today is not as safe as it was a few years ago. We cannot ignore its new dangers, leaving it up to the professionals–the police, the FBI and CIA–to take care of it. For most organizations, the focus of corporate security has been on building barriers to keep out the bad individuals. However, many of the most damaging security breaches involve employees, albeit unwittingly in most cases. "Security has to become part of the organization's DNA," says Mr. Collins of Nortel Networks, as quoted in the Economist Intelligence Unit.

Every organization is at risk. It may be difficult for us to shift our perceptions. We tend to think of the world in which we grew up as the basis of reality, and that everything else is a passing distortion of that reality. But this is only the self-centered perspective of our ego, which itself is not the center of reality. Similarly, ancient cultures viewed reality as essentially static. Although the seasons changed and although the old generations died and new generations were born, the world was like a water wheel turning in its place: winter to summer and summer to winter.

But we know that this is not true. We see how the world shifts and changes, how reality is flexible. Where we happen to have come in is immaterial. The reality that we grew up with is not any more special, not any more "real" than the reality that exists now.

We too must be flexible. We too must shift with the times. Although we need the qualities of solidity and strength, at the same time we must be quick and flexible, able to "dance like a butterfly and sting like a bee," as that very solid prize-fighter, Muhammed Ali, was fond of saying.

Today's reality includes color-coded terrorist warnings and wand searches at airports. It includes conflicts in Afghanistan and Iraq, and men who, in the name of their faith, massacre Americans. It is a reality in which we cannot afford naivete. Some people can still recall when they began to lock their doors and cars. Today we must lock the doors to our organization's resources–in particular, to its knowledge. To do so, we must begin to perceive our environment differently and our role in that environment differently.

The image of the preyed-upon small-town visitor to New York is an old cliche, and one that illustrates own our situation. The small-town visitor may be canny and able in his home town, but in a different situation he does not know the signs of danger and how to protect himself. The rules that worked at home–look a stranger in the eye, smile and say hello–do not work here. In fact, they are invitations to disaster.

In the same way, we are in a new situation with unforeseen dangers, with new rules and predators. Our old framework is as obsolete as yesterday's yellowing newspaper. We must inculcate a new state of mind and create a new corporate environment. In short, we must promulgate a "culture of security."

This "culture of security" means that the easy-going culture of openness and trust that may have characterized a company–that may have been one of its most attractive attributes–will have to be modified. And that can take place only when its workforce is educated properly, and when that education is periodically reinforced.

One reason for this is that the information explosion has changed a fundamental assumption: that the details of your business are unknown to anyone but people authorized to know those details. By way of illustration, let us take the CNA, or Customer Name and Address bureau. This is a service that the phone company maintains for authorized personnel. When someone calls the CNA and supplies a telephone number, the CNA clerk gives the customer's name and address, including unlisted the names and addresses. One time, the phone company could assume that whoever knew the CN a number was a legitimate caller. This is an application of the "security through obscurity" method: assuming that your company and its particular information are so little-known that anyone who knows it is a legitimate figure (Kevin Mitnick refers to this as well as "speakeasy security." Speakeasies were hard to find, but once you found them it was a simple matter to get past the bouncer at the door).

Nowadays, the chance that your information is secret is much smaller than it used to be. Therefore, the level of trust that you could unthinkingly extend to a voice at the other end of a phone line must be drastically curtailed (It even means nothing that your caller ID identifies someone as calling from a company phone, for this can be counterfeited).

The usual assumptions of trustworthiness must be straitened and revised. As you go hiking along the Appalachian Trail, a man wearing a backpack won't merit a second glance. A man walking with a backpack near American soldiers in Iraq is highly suspect. Assumptions about believability must be pared down. A voice over the phone is not believable (unless you recognize the voice of the person with whom you are speaking). Only when you see the company employee with whom you are talking and know him can you really trust him. Security precautions that forbid sharing information with suspect persons—even seemingly innocuous information, such as company email addresses—must be respected rigidly.

All of this is what is meant by a "culture of security." It can be difficult to implement such changes, changes that might seem burdensome, unnecessary and detrimental to the work atmosphere. Unfortunately, no business is obscure any more. No company can operate with the naivete and safety of the citizens of Mayberry, USA.

Every individual in your organization must be made aware of security risks and his or her personal security responsibilities. No one is too minor a figure in your organization, because every individual can serve as a security breach.

Promotion of such a culture of security requires leadership and extensive participation. All of the members of the organization must gain a heightened understanding of the need for security and the responsibility of every individual to be part of an intensified program of security planning and management.

In cyber-terms, a "culture of security" means that your organization systematically protects its intellectual property from all potential exposure, whether intentional or accidental, and that it minimizes the effects of any such exposure. In other words, information cannot be allowed to slip into the wrong hands. The right information must be provided to the right people at the right time. This information assurance assures the security and privacy of critical information.

Although simple in concept, information assurance involves much more than data security (the reliability, availability, integrity, accuracy and confidentiality of data) and more than protecting your computer information system from internal or external disruption. Information assurance is a systematic approach that assumes the responsibility of every individual in the organization, as well as that of every individual in all the agencies, firms and companies with which the organization interacts.

As a result of implementing a culture of security, your organization can achieve information assurance, so that its systems, networks and infrastructure (including information and communication technologies and physical facilities) will be protected.

In order to achieve information assurance, you must:

- Raise awareness about potential security risks to information systems and networks. Inform people about the policies, practices, measures and procedures to address those risks. Stress the need for their adaptation and implementation at all levels of the organization.

- Develop a set of coherent policies, practices, measures and procedures for the security of information systems and networks.

- Create a frame of reference that will help individuals understand those policies.

- Promote cooperation and appropriate information sharing among all organizational members in order to develop and implement security policies, practices, measures and procedures.

- Foster confidence among all users of information systems and networks in those systems and networks.

- Help organization members blend their security consciousness with an adherence to ethical practices.

- Place a strong emphasis on training, information assurance, contingency and continuity of operations planning, emergency and disaster preparedness, and recovery.

"The world is too much with us," complained William Wordsworth. Little did he know how much the world can intertwine itself into our most private and secure communications. But complaint is not adequate. What is needed is an awareness of the dangers and a systematic approach to information security.

Security: A Shared Responsibility

Human and technology capital are the two key components to look at when developing a business security plan. Only when both factors are dealt with in an organized and integrated fashion can security be achieved.

Both systems work together well when an entire organization has a culture of security. A system of security is pro-active, not reactive. It is flexible, not rigid: based on understanding, not rote behaviors; it asks relevant questions and has a rational methodological basis for decision-making.

To attain a culture of security, all members of an organization must enhance their awareness, education, information sharing and training.

A culture of security cannot err on the side of secrecy. Secrecy is bad for an organization because it impedes the free flow of knowledge, which is the life-blood of an organization. In addition, an organization obsessed with secrecy is no longer in consonance with the values of a free and open, democratic society. Just as the United States could not respond to the threat of terrorism by abrogating civil liberties, no organization can attempt to meet the challenge of cyber-attacks by invading employees' privacy.

The members of an organization must respect the legitimate interests of others. Given the pervasiveness of information systems and network, they must recognize that they can harm others sometimes by inappropriate activity and other time by failing to take action. All security concerns must be consonant with maintaining ethical conduct.

Such issues are not simple. For instance, as an employee, how confidential is your email? Does a supervisor have the right to monitor your Internet activity or to set up a device that tracks your every keyboard stroke and mouse click? Do you need to be apprised that your supervisor might do so? Are the files on your computer yours or the company's? Can the company monitor your phone calls or review the phone numbers that you have been dialing?

Every participant of an organization is responsible for the security of information systems and networks. Because participants' dependence upon interconnected systems and network opens them to attack, they must understand their responsibility for the security of those information systems and networks. Each member of an organization must bear some measure of accountability. Whether it is the receptionist, the CEO, the night watchman or a salesman, every individual must learn how to recognize and respond to a security threat. The threats may be on different levels of attack, yet they can each lead to serious security failures–whether that failure begins with an executive revealing confidential information or a janitor allowing into the building a man claiming to have forgotten his security pass in the car.

Through education programs, newsletters and other such means, every member of the organization must be encouraged to regularly review his or her policies, practices, measures and procedures, and assess whether they are appropriate and sufficient. Every individual must be educated as to how an intruder can gain access and how seemingly innocuous behavior can signal the commencement of a hostile attack. The forest of corporate and government security is filled with wolves who are dressed up as grandmothers.

For instance, a social engineer gets the name of an employee, Smith, in the business department. Pretending to be from the payroll department, the social engineer calls Smith and tells him that he has put through Smith's request to have his paycheck deposited directly to his credit union account. Since Smith didn't even have such an account, he is very perturbed. The social engineer asks Smith for his employee number, since payroll changes were entered by that number. So Smith gives him the number, and the social engineer reassures him that there was an error–the request was from someone else. Having acquired Smith's employee number, the social engineer calls another branch of the company pretending to be Smith, and requests a temporary account at a hotel so that he will be able to access his email without making a long distance call. As a result, the social engineer has gained access to the company's wide area network.

Every member of the organization must be educated as to the risks that threaten the organization and the safeguards that protect against those risks. This constitutes the first line of defense for the security of information systems and networks.

This campaign of education is primarily the responsibility of those who develop, design and supply products and services. They are invested with the duty to distribute information on system and network security, including regular updates to facilitate users' better understanding of their security-related responsibilities. It is best that the organization have an integrated plan of on-going education, involving those with the technical information and those responsible for organizational communication, such as the communications department, which can help organize all sorts of information campaigns.

Organizational members must be made aware of how much damage security failures may inflict. They must learn of the many ways in which a free flow of information and how the organization's interconnectivity and interdependency provide opportunities for security breaches.

Once they have been apprised of the risks, dangers and vulnerabilities, organizational members must be taught the good practices that they can implement in order to enhance security. They must learn how the company computer system works, and how to maintain current and up-to-date security practices. At the same time, they must be adhere to guidelines meant to prevent over-zealousness and the violation of others' rights.

Recognizing the interconnectivity of information systems and networks and the potential for rapid and widespread damage, participants should respond to security incidents, share information about threats and vulnerabilities, and implement procedures for rapid and effective cooperation in order to prevent, detect and respond to further security incidents.

We may think that employees of an organization are intelligent enough or have enough "street smarts" to recognize any attempt to extract information from them. But the truth is that social engineers manipulate us so skillfully that without special training and vigilance anyone of us is a likely victim.

In *The Art of Deception,* Kevin Mitnick describes a scenario in which a social engineer persuades an employee of the Social Security Administration to provide him with someone's annual income. One aspect of the social engineer's modus operandi is the use of inside information and specialized lingo that an unauthorized person would be assumed not to possess.

Mitnick notes, "Incredibly, the Social Security Administration has posted a copy of their entire Program Operations Manual on the Web, crammed with information that's useful for their people, but also incredibly valuable to social engineers. It contains abbreviations, lingo, and instructions for how to request what you want...." Mitnick goes on to give the Internet site for the manual (http://policy.ssa.gov/poms.nsf/), noting that it contains detailed information that will help one impersonate a law enforcement officer when seeking information from the SSA, "unless the agency has already read this story and removed the manual by the time you read this."

As of this date (October, 2003), the site is still online and can be reached using the address given above. A search engine for the site will guide the social engineer to all the information he needs to know about "law enforcement," and buzz words like "alphadent" and "numident."

This website still stands even though Kevin Mitnick is a man whose every word is scrutinized by law enforcement officials. Clearly, security is not about technology alone, but depends upon the human factor.

In itself technology is not impregnably secure. One of the first encrypting programs was called PGP, which stands for "Pretty Good Protection." Generally speaking, that is what security software and hardware provide. Although cryptographic programs are extremely powerful, they are often attached to machines with weak security systems. An encrypted email can make its way securely through cyberspace, but if the computer on which it is decoded is relatively insecure–if an attacker can hack the recipient's computer, read over his shoulder or go through his unshredded trash–then the encryption becomes irrelevant. All that an attacker needs is access to the weakest link. By analogy, it doesn't matter that an armed convoy of Brinks trucks is protecting the royal jewels if those jewels are delivered to a homeless man sitting on a park bench.

What works is an overlapping system of security strategies involving both technology and people that provides a reasonable measure of security. It is always better to have two different strategies than two copies of the same strategy. A bonfire burning at the entrance to a cave will keep out a sabertooth tiger. Two bonfires will be a little bit more effective. But a bonfire plus an all-night watch of men armed with spears will be much more effective. A bonfire plus an all-night watch plus some strategically-placed tiger traps will be that much more effective. The same holds for cybersecurity. Overlapping systems involving both the technological and human domains weave together to form a thick, hard-to-penetrate curtain.

What Works?

Robert A. Clyde, chief technology officer of Symantec Corporation, states that computer "attacks [against organizations] are getting more frequent, and they are more complex. Companies can't just keep throwing money at the last attack…They need to get more proactive and put together a more holistic program that will protect them against tomorrow's attack."

When you buy a burglar alarm for your house, you can judge its capabilities in a number of ways. You can look at all of the functions that it provides: voice alarm, police notification, movement sensors, and so forth. You can look at how user-friendly it is: movement-activated video camera at the front door, easy-to-understand interface, voice commands, and so forth. You can see how effective each of its functions is. For instance, does the movement detector go off every time a curtain rustles or, on the other hand, does it not notice when someone crawls through the room?

However, let us look at your house from the viewpoint of a burglar. He goes by your house and sees a sign on your lawn: "Acme House Security." Now he knows what kind of system you are using. He is interested not in the functionality of its particular features, but in what he can do to rob you. What are its weakest links and how can they be compromised? Or, alternatively, how can he circumvent the system altogether?

Let's say he knows exactly where your jewels are. He knows that he can get in and out of your house with your jewels within half a minute. To such a burglar, it doesn't matter very much that he will set off the alarm. By the time the neighbors get aroused and the police arrive, he will be gone. Or he can circumvent the alarm altogether by posing as the gas man. He can use a ladder to break in through an unsecured second floor window. He can find a way to repeatedly set off false alarms (each time causing the police to come to your house) so that you will eventually turn the alarm off.

Your organization's security situation is no different. What counts is not your security devices' particular functions, but rather how your organization is protected overall. Having a culture of security means that you look at the totality of your system and at how an attacker thinks. It is our tendency to set up a protective device and then limit our thinking to how strong that device is. But an attacker won't waste his time on that. If your house has Medco locks, the attacker won't bother about them if your windows are unsecured. Even if your house has a police notification system, the attacker won't be concerned about it if your electricity goes out every time there is a rainstorm.

Most of us are not larcenous and it can be difficult–it can even feel opprobrious–to take on the mind-set of an attacker. But that is what security consciousness demands. If you were coming to attack your own organization's system, what would you do? If you know that, then you know what is weak and what needs to be fixed.

Police officials state that one of the most effective deterrents to a burglar is the presence of a dog. Why is a dog's presence even more effective than that of a burglar alarm? A dog is constantly alert and suspicious. It is hard to turn him off. The dog is loud and obstinate. He will not easily go away. And the dog is dangerous. He will attack and cause injury.

What does this mean in terms of your company's security? It means, first of all, that live security personnel can often protect your security in ways that technological mechanisms cannot.

And it also means that "a good offense is the best defense." When you take a purely defensive stance, then you are giving an attacker a great advantage. Your organization is visible, but your attacker is invisible. Your attacker can study your organization and its security at length, taking all the time that he needs. You, on the other hand, only have access to him during the limited time that he is visible to you. You have to protect a complex system with many potential points of entry, but he needs only to find and exploit one of those links.

Also, if at all possible, make it costly for anyone attacking your system. This may not always be easy, particularly if your attacker is launching a cyber-attack from overseas and you cannot even identify him, much less extradite and convict him. But the more power that an organization has to harm those who attempt to harm it, the more secure it will be. A burglar alarm can irritate a burglar's ears. A large dog can make it impossible for him to function and cause him serious bodily injury. Which is he more likely to avoid?

Is It Worth It?

When, if ever, is maintaining a "culture of security" unreasonable? For instance: is it unreasonable to lock your door because a locked door is bothersome when you return from the store with an arm load of groceries? Or is it unreasonable to check everyone's identity every time they enter a corporation building because it annoys the executives?

The answer to these questions is: it depends. In regard to locking your door, it depends on whether you live in a town in North Dakota with a population of 44 or in Dallas, Texas. In regard to checking IDs, it depends on what the organization has worth stealing, what the odds are that someone will sneak into the building, and how bad the morale amongst the executives is.

Taking individual circumstances into account, it is reasonable to say that every corporation can and should adopt new practices. One the one hand, it is not reasonable to adopt every defensive posture just because it is available. But to make do without any is as irresponsible as a young person hitchhiking because "most people are good."

In Tennessee Williams' *A Streetcar Named Desire*, Blanche declared, "I have always depended upon the kindness of strangers." Our new cyber-reality means that more than ever we are in the midst of strangers. Depending upon their kindness is a poor strategy in the best of times.

The "culture of security" is not an unreasonable expectation nor an onerous burden. We human beings are remarkably flexible and can adapt quickly to a variety of situations. Adopt the particulars of "the culture of security" that make sense for your organization. You will find that the initial discomforts that they cause will be far outweighed by the security that they provide.

CHAPTER FOUR

KNOWLEDGE AND SECURITY

The Damage Done

The security of knowledge refers to how well an organization protects its knowledge from hostile incursions. We have already discussed who makes unauthorized use of knowledge and some of the uses they make of it.

Here, we will go on to discuss various ways that companies can protect themselves against those who steal and manipulate knowledge.

Consider how much damage is done (or at least reported) every year. In 2003, for instance, 251 respondents to a Computer Security Institute survey responded that they had suffered over $20 million in financial losses due to attack or misuse of computer, the four chief causes being theft of proprietary information ($71 million), denial of service ($66 million), viruses ($27 million) and insider abuse of Internet access ($12 million). We are used to glancing at such figures and allowing our eyes to glaze over. But if we take a moment to look at and think about these figures, we will see that they are truly staggering. The amount of financial damage done through cyber-crime is truly extraordinary. The amount of money that could be saved if not for the depredation of computer-crime would be enough to run a small country.[1]

---

[1] For the details of this survey and other survey results, see Appendix B at the end of the book.

Computer Attacks

Here we will list the most common computer security threats and then steps that you can take to protect your enterprise.

1. Viruses

Viruses are computer programs that are designed to replicate themselves and infect computers when triggered by a specific event. A macro virus is activated every time a macro runs, such as an automatic routine that sends email. A virus can only affect a computer after it enters through an outside source–usually an attachment to an email or a file downloaded from the Internet. Viruses range from completely benign to maliciously destructive.

2. Trojan Horse

A Trojan horse comes hidden in some harmless software program (just as the Greeks entered Troy hidden in a wooden horse). A Trojan horse can inflict a great deal of damage, such as deletion data. A Trojan horse can be contracted only after it enters through an outside source–usually an email attachment or a file downloaded from the Internet.

3. Back Door Program

This is often installed by a Trojan horse. A back door (also known as a remote administration program) allows intruders access into and control of your computer.

4. Attacks

- **Reconnaissance Attack**

A reconnaissance attack uses software tools such as *sniffers* and *scanners* to gather information that is used only later to compromise networks (as well as home computers).

- **Access Attack**

An access attack breaks into your email account, database and other confidential information.

- **Denial of Service Attack**

A denial of service attack overwhelms a computer connected to the Internet with a great deal of junk data, thus blocking legitimate traffic. In a distributed denial of service attack, an attacker compromises multiple machines or hosts. In other words, a cyber-criminal can take over hundreds of computers to launch a denial of service attack.

5. Data Interception

Perpetrators can read email or other data transmitted via any type of network, and even alter it. In IP spoofing, a perpetrator's site mimics that of a legitimate data recipient. It is as though someone built a house with your address in order to steal your mail.

6. Corrupted Mobile Code

Intruders can use "mobile code" (such as Java, JavaScript and ActiveX) to gather information on you or to run malicious code on your computer.

7. Cross-Site Scripting

When a website responds to a message from you, it unwittingly transfers a malicious script to your browser. You can contract this merely by following links in web pages, email messages or newsgroup postings.

8. Email Spoofing

Spoofed email is merely email with a forged return address. By pretending to be someone you know, someone sending such email can try to get you to reveal some confidential material, such as stating your password.

9. Physical Theft

Your computer might contain significant and private information. If your computer is stolen, all of that information might be compromised.

10. Scams

Scams can be as obvious as a businessman in Nigeria who will, for a reasonable fee, allow you to share in the proceeds of a multi-million dollar bank account, and as subtle as a program that steals the personal information that you type into an ostensibly secure form on a truly legitimate website.

11. Spam

Although essentially a nuisance, spam takes up bandwidth and wastes time. Particularly obnoxious spam, such as invitations to view pornography sites, can be damaging to young people.

Security Tools and Techniques

1. Anti-Virus Software

Anti-virus software is a desideratum on every computer. Anti-virus software must be updated continuously, and many software packages automatically update themselves every time you log onto the Internet.

2. Anti-Spyware Software

This software helps ensures that no one is tracking your Internet usage or copying your keystrokes into your computer.

3. Passwords

The sophistication and strength of programs meant to break passwords is beyond most people's awareness. Certainly it does not suffice to use a default password or a host of easy passwords that a hacker can guess at, such as "password," the name of someone in your family, your address, your phone number, and so forth. Today programs can run at top speed, trying every word in the dictionary, anagrams and combinations of words, numbers and typographical symbols. The best advice is to choose a long password including letters, numbers, capital letters and typographical symbols. However, be reasonable: don't choose a password that is so difficult that you have to tape it to your computer console. In addition, change your password on a regular basis.

4. Firewalls

A firewall is "a system or group of systems that enforces an access control policy between two networks" (Firewalls FAQ). A firewall can be a piece of software or hardware. Like a lock on a door, permits only authorized users to enter your network–at least, theoretically. But be aware that determined intruders see firewalls as a challenge, not as a barrier.

5. Email Attachments

Don't open email attachments from unknown sources. Be suspicious even if the attachment comes from a friend. Often, people unwittingly pass along attachments that have been infected by a virus, such as the "I Love You Virus," which affected millions of people.

6. File Sharing

Unless you really need it, turn off the file-sharing feature on your network. This will limit the access that a stranger can have to your computer.

7. Back Up

A simple way to protect your knowledge data is to back it up regularly. At least once a week, back it up onto a CD, and every day back up individual files onto floppy disks.

8. Download

Regularly download security "patches." Unfortunately, there are so many patches for so many software applications that, practically speaking, this is not very good advice. And even when a patch is available, it is often of questionable quality and difficult to install.

9. Evaluate

Evaluate your computer security at least twice a year–perhaps at the same time that you make sure that your smoke detector has a good battery.

10. Disconnect

Disconnect from the Internet when not in use. The longer you remain on the Internet, the more of a target to you present to cyber-criminals. This is particularly pertinent for those who have DSL connection, which is generally never disconnected.

What Do Cyber-Criminals Do?

The list of crimes that an intruder can commit is unfortunately quite long. They can:

- Read your email
- Send out forged email using your name
- Examine the material on your computer
- Use your computer as a base from which to attack other systems, such as government or financial systems
- Take down enough information from your computer to steal your identity, reformat your hard drive, change your data
- Change your computer's system configurations
- Read, steal or alter documents on your computer
- Infect your computer with a virus

Fortunately, the steps that you can take to protect yourself are quite extensive. Let us have a look at some of the weaknesses inherent in a computer network and at some of the ways that you can strengthen your network.

Strengthening Your Network–A Checklist

1. Your Network Perimeter

Your network perimeter refers to those nodes where your network interfaces with the world at large, in the same way that the doors to your office building allow traffic in and out.

How do you police those doors? You can post a security guard who will demand some form of identification: an ID card, a time-based token, a combination of some of these things.

Similarly, how do you secure your network perimeter? You set up a firewall, which is designed to keep unauthorized users out of your network.

How can an unauthorized person get past the guard and into your office building? He can blend in with a group of legitimate office workers and insinuate his way in. He can befriend an employee, who will escort him in. He can find a backdoor entrance where there is no guard or where the guard is not particularly alert.

Similarly, there are ways that a determined attacker can get past your firewall. One way is the equivalent of befriending an employee and having that employee help him get in. Although your firewall may be secure, your computer applications that are open to the Internet, such as your webserver software or computer operating system (such as Windows) may have flaws that will allow a hacker into your network. The recent Blaster worm (a type of computer virus) insinuated its way into computer networks through a flaw in Windows.

This is like a medieval castle with a huge, fortified door. Next to that door is a little door where a guard is stationed. As an attacker, you don't need to worry about the huge door. If you bribe the guard, he will let you and all of your friends in through the little door. You could take over and destroy the entire castle without ever once worrying about its formidable perimeter defenses.

But how prevalent are such software flaws that can allow attackers to sneak into your system? The answer is that they are extraordinarily common. There are so many, in fact, that it becomes a practical impossibility for any organization to protect against all of them, to reliably update all software with "patches" meant to stem software vulnerabilities. Software companies are in a hurry to get their products out and it has become the norm to release "buggy" products and repair them in response to user complaints. This is somewhat analogous to a car company putting out a car whose brakes, steering, wheel alignment, air bags, seat belts, carburetor, transmission, belts, and body strength have not yet been tested in actual road conditions, with the philosophy that the most effective way to learn about the car's weaknesses is to have a million people drive it.

Because there is no realistic way to repair all software flaws (just as you couldn't buy a car and then bring it into the shop three times a day to repair newly-discovered flaws), networks are often attacked by problems for which a "patch" has already been provided. For instance, Blaster struck a full month after Microsoft had already provided a patch to repair the flaw that Blaster exploited. In 2002, Symantec Corporation documented 2,524 new software flaws, most of them "severe," and more than half of which were classified as "easy to exploit."

Another way that attackers can make their way through the network perimeter is to exploit employees' naivete and carelessness about computer security. This often occurs when employees bend company rules about inconvenient computer security. For instance, an employee may connect his home computer to the company network or download software, such as chat programs, which can provide a means for viruses to enter your network.

File-sharing programs are also culprits. For instance, if a user installs KaZaA (a music file swapping network), incorrectly, he gives access to anyone else on the globe to a good part of his computer system. Anyone can go on the KaZaA network, type appropriate words into a keyword search and turn up memos of company decisions, personnel evaluations and the like.

How do you protect your network perimeter? Two simple things you can do are to install a firewall that blocks file sharing and turn off software features that you are not using in order to minimize the possibility of software bugs being exploited.

2. Email

Email is the most well-known medium for transporting viruses and their cousins. Yet, despite that fact that computer users have been warned for years about the dangers of opening email attachments, they continue to do so, and viruses of an increasing virulence continue to infect millions of computers across the globe, sending entire systems crashing and causing billions of dollars worth of damage. Whereas viruses originally did little more than deliver a prankish message or cause some relatively minor damage, today's more malevolent viruses can settle onto your computer, record all of your keystrokes and then file them away for a hacker to come and pick them up at his leisure. Such a program that has been snuck into your system is a Trojan horse. One type of email attachment installs a program that will re-route your Internet access through an overseas phone number, which will show up on your phone bill as a hefty sum. Other viruses (as well as "legitimate" programs such as KaZaA) will install spyware on your computer, which will track your Internet activity and report on it to a central data base, usually used by companies collecting data in order to sell you products. Altogether, there are close to 65,000 known viruses loose (most of which affect Windows PCs, and of which about 100 are directed at Apple Macintosh computers).

The defense against such email attacks is straightforward: use an anti-virus program, preferably one that automatically updates itself from the Internet. These programs will, among other things, block spyware, which you can also block using a freeware product called Ad-Aware. It can also be helpful to setup email filters that block attached files of a type commonly used to transmit viruses, e.g., executable programs with filename extensions such as .exe and .pif.

3. Web Sites

Your web site, your face to the world, is also liable to attack–ranging from defacement of your site, an annoying although relatively benign attack, to attacks that cause serious damage. Some attacks are meant to close your system down–so-called "denial of service" attacks, which can be very hard to defend against. Other, more commercially minded bandits, are interested in stealing information that can be financially remunerative, such as customers' information.

How can you protect yourself against such abuses? First of all, put a firewall in place separating your web site from your database. This will prevent attackers from coming in and stealing customers' credit card information and the like, which they use directly, sell to others, or even sell back to the company from which they stole it. According to Chris Wysopal, director of research and development at @stake, Inc., you can remove 50 per cent of the threat of web attacks simply by stripping down your web server, deactivating all of the functions that you don't need.

4. Remote Users

A chain is only as strong as its weakest link. If remote users can get onto your site, they are probably that weak link. An attacker can access a remote site and deliver an attack.

A woman can work at a thoroughly secure company, but if she takes her laptop home and uses it for file sharing, that security is compromised. Home computers are frequently used to piggy-back into secure networks. This is because many home computers are easy for hackers to access, particularly if, using DSL or cable connections, these Internet connections are continuously on, thus providing a steady target. In addition, home computers are often not maintained securely, particularly if they are being shared with one's children who might be downloading files and other software indiscriminately.

No matter how careful the organization is to maintain security, that responsibility ultimately resides with the remote user. For instance, the organization may elect to use a virtual private network, or VPN, which provides a secure link between itself and a remote user. But if the remote PC has been compromised, the hacker will simply ride with it into the organization's network. As Nir Zuk, a chief technology officer at NetScreen Technologies, states, "The easiest way to target your enterprise is through a telecommuter who's not as well protected as the enterprise."

Because instructing remote users about the proper protocols and precautions they should take may be in vain, some companies use a program to scan the computer of any remote user attempting to log on and reject any computer that is not configured in accordance with network security standards.

5. The Corrupt Insider

The corrupt insider is a corrosive and frightening problem, because an insider by definition must be allowed into your system. If the FBI, CIA and other top security agencies have entrusted information upon whose lives agents depended to employees who betrayed that information, how can you keep these bad guys out of your company?

There are no assurances in this world. But there are ways to reduce the likelihood of hiring such people and of mitigating the threat of insider abuse. A first step is to carefully screen prospective employees. The next is to monitor computer use for illicit activity and to limit all employees from information that is not relevant to them. Finally, as soon as an employee leaves the firm, his or her access to the network must be terminated, and ID badge, electronic access device and so forth must be returned. If the employee had access to particularly sensitive material or is particularly suspect, you might even want all of his former colleagues to change their passwords.

6. Telephone

Jeff Miller, network security officer at Old National Bankcorp in Evansville, Indiana, states that "a single modem dialing up an ISP can basically go around $100,000 of firewalling equipment." No matter how well you secure the link between your company and the Internet, it takes just one employee using an unprotected modem to compromise your organization's entire network.

Hackers roam the Internet using freely-available software called "war dialers," which can detect, among other things, which phone lines being used by a corporation are modems, and then focus on them until they find an unprotected modem.

Another technique that hackers use is to break into a company's "public branch exchange," or PBX (this is known as PBX phreaking), and utilize it to place expensive, unauthorized calls or to sell access to some other party.

To protect against the abuse of unauthorized modems, your company can use the same technology that the hackers use: employ a war dialer to ascertain that all of the modems on your network are protected. Specially constructed firewalls will prevent the misuse of PBX's.

7. Wireless Fidelity (Wi Fi)

Wireless Fidelity is a technology that allows workers in a company to connect to the company network or through the network into the Internet without having to plug into any sockets. Of course, so can anyone else in the vicinity who has access to a computer, including a hacker parked at the curb. Setting up a wireless fidelity system without security safeguards is akin to broadcasting your most private files and information on a radio signal accessible to anyone driving by with a car radio installed.

Fortunately, there are effective means of preventing such eavesdropping.

First, use a firewall to prevent outsiders from listening in. Take care that the firewall is not set up around your wireless fidelity system. If it is, then you are basically allowing any passerby the ability to circumvent the firewall. It is akin to digging a moat around your castle and then inviting your armed attackers in so that they can take a free and unguided tour of your facilities.

Also, use automatic encryption devices that will prevent unauthorized users from getting into your network and reading confidential emails.

Run a user-authentication program to keep unauthorized users out of your system.

And finally, to maintain control over security, introduce and enforce a policy preventing organization members from setting up unauthorized and unprotected access points (which employees are liable to do for simple convenience' sake).

8. Encryption

Encryption means to make something "cryptic"–hidden or secret. Presumably, the person engaged in encryption wants to seal information away, like a body in a crypt. What is encryption used for, and how does it operate?

Encryption can be used for a number of processes that are central to the theme of computer security.

- Keeps email correspondence (ordinarily as open as a postcard) a secret from any on-lookers.
- Assures the recipient of electronic information that it comes from whom it claims to come, and that it has not been altered on the way.
- Makes it impossible for two parties to correspondence (such as a contract) deny their role assures security in electronic commerce.
- Assures the authenticity of an electronic document.

Encryption, in short, takes regular text (plaintext), stamps its identity and makes it opaque to anyone but the correct user.

How does it do that? Encryption must rely on more than a simple code, such as letter substitution. And it must rely on more than an ordinary password, even a somewhat sophisticated one. You might think that !PrettySmart*DudE is an unbreakable code. But in 1999, a keysearch project (on distributed.net) utilized a machine that was able to test 250 billion keys per second. This technique, called *brute force,* will chew up any ordinary password in short order.

Therefore, to encode documents, cryptographers use long and complex algorithms. Theoretically, these too could be cracked, but the best algorithms would take today's technology a millennium to achieve that task–by which time, we can assume, the information would have grown obsolete.

The mathematics are impeccable. But because our world consists of more than pure mathematics, encryption is not impeccably assured. As mentioned earlier, a poor password is a weak defense. A poor password used to access an encryption program brings to power of the entire program down to the level of the password. Even when algorithms are used, any regularity to the flow of numbers is something that can be exploited by an encryption-cracking program. Some companies use such questionable algorithms. Avoid them, for patterns are vulnerable.

By way of analogy, think of a lock. The average lock has five pins, each of which can be in one of ten different positions: leading to a total possibility of 100,000 different positions. Theoretically, if you wanted to open the door but had lost your key, you would need to try up to 100,000 keys (you could also smash the lock, but that's a different story). In reality, however, each manufacturer's locks have certain shared characteristics–they are not entirely random. Thus, a locksmith does not need more than a dozen or so keys to open any lock by that manufacturer (although he may need to force the lock, to some extent).

Nevertheless, encryption programs are very powerful and in many cases indispensable. No company can conduct on-line commerce without providing security, which in turn is provided by the tools of encryption.

If your organization is considering acquiring encryption tools, it cannot do so thoughtlessly. It must go through a thorough analysis of what it needs, what an encryption program offers, and whether what the program offers is economically viable. Throughout the process, those making decisions must be careful to keep in the forefront of their thinking what their business needs. It is easy to get carried away with the capabilities of an encryption program and set aside the questions of whether those dazzling capabilities answer the needs of the organization.

Public Key Infrastructure (PKI) is an infrastructure that provides capabilities for digital signature and digital encryption. There are several good PKI solutions available, and implementations vary with the nature of the business transactions being supported. Building a business solution around a specific technology is a common pitfall. So when choosing a PKI system, focus on the functional capabilities (digital signing and encryption) you need rather than the PKI's features.

The core functions that PKI provides are *authentication*, *authorization* and *confidentiality*.

Authentication is the means of establishing the identity of an entity. Authentication is necessary to ensure that electronic transactions are being conducted between known parties. When strong authentication is established, the security characteristic of "non-repudiation" is present. "Non-repudiation" means that neither party involved in the transaction can plausibly deny that they were involved. The technology provides the "eye-witness account" that the transaction occurred.

Authorization associates an authenticated entity with a list of permitted (authorized) actions. These two elements of authentication and authorization work together to bind a transaction with an approval. The specific nature of the binding depends on how the business application integrates with the PKI.

The following example demonstrates authentication and authorization:

Employees at company XYZ access their pay statements and information on-line. Part of the application positively authenticates each user uniquely. Strict access control is necessary to ensure that unauthorized persons cannot gain access to personal pay records.

The application also includes the function to permit employees to change payroll assignments (e.g., 401(k) contribution allotments). Once a change is made to payroll information, the application must be able to do the following:

- Prove who accessed the payroll information and when;
- Prove what changes were made;
- Archive the transaction record for a specified period of time and be able to prove, with a high degree of assurance, that an authorized entity conducted a legitimate transaction.

Confidentiality relates to the function that ensures that information and transaction are disclosed only those involved in the exchange. Only authorized entities are permitted to "see" the transaction. The term *entity* is used to represent the possibilities that a transaction may occur between two users, a user and a process (such as an application), between two devices, or between two or more processes (application to application exchange).

The first step in analyzing requirements for digital signing and encryption is to ignore the technology and focus on business needs. Some key questions to ask are:

- Are the transactions all electronic except for a legacy print function that requires paper filing of a signed document?
- Is the volume of transactions expected or desired to significantly increase?
- Is there an electronic signature solution in place that appends a transaction with an ID code representing authorization?

Electronic transactions should be divided into at least three types: internal users (i.e. employees), trusted partners and unknown users. As the transactions are extended from trusted partners to unknown users, the complexity of the management function significantly increases.

The volume of transactions and processing time is critical to business concerns. One way to increase volume is to decrease the processing time for each transaction. One way to do this is to replace a shipment of physical documents with an electronic transfer.

Trust relationships can prove extremely difficult to establish and maintain. Electronically, there should be a traceable chain-of-trust linking the transaction to its participants. Any occurrence of a gap or a data-handling function within the transaction stream potentially increases the complexity. Legislation or policy may exist that dictates the nature of a "signature" or of an "authorization." In other cases, regulations may be silent on the technical means.

In deciding what PKI to deploy, ask the following questions:

- Are there business transactions and processes that require signatures from established, authorized personnel?
- Is the transaction currently automated (e.g., EDI transaction)?
- What is the nature of the trust relationships in terms of numbers, access to technology and trust?
- What are current policy and legislation issues governing the business process?

The purpose of these questions is to clarify the nature of the current business, in order to assure that using a PKI will demonstrate an improvement worth the cost of implementation.

The business case for adapting a PKI system will have to demonstrate how the cost of implementation will provide a return on investment. For example, the deployment of PKI may open new service markets, enable new services (e.g., self-serve applications), or automate and hasten current processes such as claim-processing time.

When estimating costs, take into account initial investigative work and planning. Some capital investment and procurement processes will be necessary. Transition costs may involve running two concurrent technologies (legacy and updated system) simultaneously. Transition costs may also include some business process re-engineering. In addition, recurring operational and maintenance costs (including training) will have to be considered.

Organizations should avoid simply replicating a business process electronically. Rather, they should re-examine how they can gain in efficiency through the use of technology.

The business analysis should address:

- The functional business requirements
- The advantages and disadvantages (with established metrics) in order to make a reasonable evaluation of options
- Identification of any business processes that will have to change or be re-evaluated
- Market analysis of similar industries that have implemented systems/processes
- A list of at least three options, with one recommended approach

Assuming that the organization opts to proceed, it should proceed with a pilot program. The purpose of the pilot program is to establish a quick success that will demonstrate new capabilities, gain organizational support, educate users and form the basis of the larger implementation. The pilot will also be used to select and evaluate a chosen technology. Therefore, the pilot should begin with strict operational target objectives that can be measured and evaluated.

By strictly adhering to functional specifications supporting specific business drivers, the organization will avoid the pitfall of building its business around a product. Instead, the product should support the business.

Few organizations have the discipline to create a throwaway or prototype. The prototype usually becomes the core of the new system. Therefore, the pilot system should demonstrate all of the end-system functionality. Initial architectural design will have to incorporate the expansion goals of the system's postpilot implementation.

Pilot implementation should include both a formalized Preliminary Design Review and Critical Design Review (PDR and CDR). The outcome of these two reviews should reduce the costs of the final implementation. At the same time, the pilot should be able to demonstrate some cost savings for the capital investment by the organization. Demonstrating cost savings will help maintain project momentum for the full implementation.

When organizations successfully implement a pilot and realize their business objectives, little stands in the way of achieving the major implementations. A lot of work remains and good project management skills will play an important role in the building and deployment phases.

It is critical to ensure that system testing and quality assurance processes are in place at every stage of development, in order to ensure that the deployed system meets requirements. During the design and building phase, organizations should work on training for the deployment. Large-scale rollouts can make training and transition issues highly complex.

The most common mistakes organizations make is to depart from a systems engineering approach. Short-shifting requirements analysis or rushing pilot development may reduce initial costs, but will cause significant schedule delays and cost over-runs when re-engineering efforts are included.

Don't involve product vendors until after all functional business objectives and processes have been evaluated. The functional design should include only products that have been pre-determined. For example, a legacy database or specific system interface definitions are constants. Involving product vendors too soon can result in subjective technology evaluations that may unnecessarily complicate the project.

Probably the most critical element to the entire process is the development of a representative, functional (not necessarily "fully functional") pilot so that the organization can see how the system is going to support business objectives.

9. Hello, IPv6

There is a technology development on the horizon that will have important ramifications in protecting computer networks against attack. But here, as in all other areas, its effectiveness will dependent on how well those in charge of networks and systems set it up and take care of it.

Protecting IT assets from both internal and external threats is the *raison d'etre* of Information Assurance (IA). Those in the Information Security business know and understand this premise quite well and are constantly challenged to keep apprised of evolutionary developments–be they environmental, social, cultural or technical. This is important because such developments, if not fully understood or adequately prepared for, can affect IA's ability to protect clients.

One such technological development is the advent of Internet Protocol Version 6 (IPv6). IPv6 is the replacement for the current method (IPv4) the world uses for assigning addresses to computers and other devices that connect to the Internet. This is your computer's electronic address much as your home and office have addresses. In order for computers to communicate, they must have a unique and distinct address.

The IPv4 addressing implementation uses a mere 32 bits (1s and 0s) to provide 4 billion addresses for use worldwide. IPv6 will increase our address neighborhood to approximately 35 trillion possible addresses by increasing the number of 1s and 0s (bits) used for addressing from 32 to 128.

Do we need more address space? Are we already running out of the 4 billion possible addresses? Even though the Internet has only been around since 1969, and some iteration of IP was introduced in the early 1980s, that may be the case. Connections to the Internet have exploded in part due to the advent of the wireless revolution and the technological advancements enabling almost anything to be Internet-capable. IPv6 was developed to handle this expansion.

With the addressing capacity of IPv6, *everything* can and probably will be part of the Internet. At the Information Assurance level, the ubiquitous copier machine can already be equipped with an address for networking purposes. And other than the recommended practical security advice of "make sure to promptly retrieve anything you copy," little attention is paid to a copier being hacked and its data compromised or corrupted. IPv6 can enable us to give addresses not only to our copiers but every other device throughout our client's enterprises.

The trade press recently has been rife with articles heralding the coming of IPv6. Recently, the Defense Department issued a memorandum mandating transition to IPv6 for all networking by fiscal year 2008. The armed services have issued implementation guidance and are in the process of identifying all IT assets that will have to comply with the Defense Department directive.

What are the overall ramifications for computer and network security professionals? For network security professionals, the paradigm of network protection will greatly shift–especially under the impetus of the wireless movement. That, coupled with IPv6, will expand the concept of protecting a "network." This growth will occur because of IPv6's operational ease of use.

IPv6 is touted as being more secure than IPv4. Unlike IPv4, IPv6 theoretically makes end-to-end security a reality. Other features include "sparsely populated address spaces (that) render it highly resistant to malicious scans and inhospitable to automated scanning and self-propagating worms and hybrid threats." However, this feature is diminished in the case of poorly designed networks. The technical advantage of auto-configuration can allow a successful intruder to penetrate the system by means of such items as "rogue routers," among others. And it will be possible to employ IPv6 wherever it is implemented, even before other, commensurate sites have upgraded from IPv4.

The fly in the ointment of the security proclamations is–as it always has been–the untrained, not-so-security-conscious administrator/implementer and unlicensed programmer.

For example, IPv6 cannot protect against the harassed and overworked administrator or user who is behind on patches and updates and who, in his or her haste to bring a server on-line, implements a less-than-correctly-configured server. Many administrators are unaware that their networks and systems are already IPv6 capable. Hackers know that and reports are surfacing that they are beginning to explore the possibilities and exploit this ignorance. Additionally, companies will need the traditional and effective network and host protection. While IPv6 is now in (limited) use and some implementation has begun, little has surfaced concerning the wide testing and deployment required to catch the bugs that are inherently and unfortunately present in any new iteration of things technological.

The implementation of IPv6 will no doubt have a major impact on both our personal lives and professional endeavors. Yet our society does not require licenses for programmers or developers. Thus we will continue to be subject to developers of new technologies whose credentials, experience and efforts–despite the large impact on us–are not subject to governmental oversight or exacting professional common standards.

Much of the cyber-world runs on Microsoft. Its products permeate the fabric of our society. On Microsoft's TechNet site, where it lists the security features for its IPv6 iteration included with Microsoft Windows Server 2003, it also lists Ipv6's security limitations, which are significant. Thus we are back to relying on the knowledge and talents of the overworked and often not-so-security-conscious administrator or implementer. In addition, Microsoft warns of other significant weak points that may result in failure of the system. Microsoft, however, does provide fairly solid recommendations to mitigate these already identified weaknesses.

According to an article in the Intercepts section of Federal Computer Week (August 11, 2003), the Defense Department will require extensive help from its industry partners as it moves to IPv6, and confirms that all new networks plugging into the Defense Department Global Information Gig (GIG) after October 1, 2003 must be IPv6 compatible. The Defense Department will need help not only with the proper implementation of IPv6 but also with the security issues that its implementation will raise.

In short, IPv6 is coming. The Internet will become even more omnipresent as everything from copiers to fax machines becomes IP-enabled, and the resulting impact on our daily, personal and professional lives will be great. There will be turmoil in some sectors and increased and different security incidents. The key to a successful transition is awareness of the technical and security issues, addressing solutions beforehand and continued advocacy for security professionalization and licensing of the administrator and implementer workforce.

Situational Awareness

Military personnel, especially USAF fighter pilots, routinely receive specialized and situational awareness training in order to enhance their survivability in the battle space and their ability to achieve overcome the adversary. Effective situational awareness helps these combatants recognize, process and fully understand their information environment.

Maintaining situational awareness is also applicable to network security professionals. It is often the overlooked security skill. Although the consequences of poor situational awareness faced by the fighter pilot (i.e., possible death) are unlikely in the cyber world of network security, other consequences could include compromise of sensitive mission information (confidentiality), corruption of vital operational data (integrity) and even denial of service of networks and computer systems (availability). Further, such consequences can consist of a violation of federal laws.

Protecting a client's electronic information records and databases is one of the most important business services an IA professional provides for securing an enterprise. Based upon formal risk assessments, cyber-security professionals maintain strategic and tactical situational awareness through constant vigilance and reevaluation of identified threats and vulnerabilities during normal and anomalous operational conditions.

Because of its dynamic nature, situational awareness is hard to maintain and extremely easy to lose. Constantly keeping on top of it is difficult at best for any cyber-warrior, especially during complex high stress operations. Maintaining situational awareness is not an easy task, since loss can often be attributed to basic common flaws in human nature, and can happen to even the most experienced network defender. Consider only two human frailties:

- **Information Overload**. The human brain, although still arguably the most efficient computer in use today, has finite limitations on how quickly and efficiently it processes input. This processing rate naturally varies between individuals and is complicated by such variables as emotional states and training. As a result, saturation can occur very quickly during cyber-attacks. The result is often less than optimum command and control decision-making.
- **Myopic View.** Under stress, combatants often focus to the point where only a narrow view of ongoing events exists because of reliance on a single data stream to the exclusion of others. This can result in a failure to think ahead for possible future ramifications.

In addition, situational awareness can be lost or misperceived by individuals using incorrect or unapproved procedures in dealing with a situation, imprecise perception of events, complacency, failing to adhere to policies, instructions or regulations and failing to resolve discrepancies early. For example, when different sources of data conflict, network security personnel sometimes fail to resolve the issue at the outset and it can have a snowball effect, again leading to bad decision making.

During the Renaissance, the poet John Donne penned, "No man is an island." The pervasiveness of the Internet has made this quote especially germane when we consider the diverse and geographically separated information infrastructures of many organizations, both corporate and governmental. Routine coordination, communication and information sharing with counterparts at all enterprise activities greatly enhance the situational awareness required to secure the entire enterprise.

Constant vigilance and routine monitoring of all technical components within the enterprise are a direct input to good situational awareness. Problems at one facility, identified through coordination and communication, can potentially be a problem at another.

Another prerequisite for situational awareness is being a professional expert at an assigned task and being cognizant of the duty responsibilities of others involved in protecting the enterprise. For example, the individual who scans packets generated by an Intrusion Detection system may not have to be technically savvy on the duties and responsibilities of the Information Security Officer or System Administrator. However, knowing the general tasks of all players in the enterprise can enhance overall situational awareness by providing input from various areas of expertise.

Effective cyber-warriors are constantly aware of the mission, its goals and progress. Any activity that causes deviations in accomplishing the mission should send an alarm and cause instant reassessment of the situation.

Situational awareness is vitally dependent upon information. Within an organization there are numerous briefings such as daily updates, shift-change briefings for 24-hour operations, etc. To help ensure the enterprise remains secure, those tasked with protecting networks and systems need to attend all appropriate briefings, pay attention and take notes. This is especially true after coming back from time off.

World events often have direct ramifications on the workloads and focus of information security professionals at every level. For example, planned U.S. actions overseas often result in spikes of scanning or other potentially harmful activities on U.S. military and corporate networks. Keeping apprised of civilian sector, government and military news can increase situational awareness and result in increased vigilance for those types of attempts on enterprise systems and networks.

Professionals subscribe to sites hosted by cyber response organizations such as the CERT Coordination Center (CERT/CC), Forum for Incident Response and Security Teams, Computer Incident Advisory Capability (CIAC), the Defense Department Cert, Infraguard and the appropriate military CERT. These organizations often compile and report ongoing computer incidents as well as maintain repositories of past events.

An IA professional must report any and all suspected events and incidents to the appropriate higher echelon. Part of situational awareness is collecting the smaller parts from a myriad of sources to deliver the big picture.

During wartime, opposing commanders send out patrols to probe the enemy's lines looking for weaknesses in defenses to attack. The electronic version of this activity is routinely done today against our networks and systems. The IA professional must watch incoming network traffic, pay particular attention to *all* probes. Probes can be precursors to other, more serious things to come.

Cyber-Karate

Brad Powell, a member of the Sun Microsystems GESS Global Security Team, states that "security is not something you buy. It is not a product (no matter what vendors try to tell you). Security is something you *live*. I often compare it to martial arts training. Just because you have achieved a black belt doesn't mean you stop training; on the contrary, you have learned from your training that it takes discipline, attitude, philosophy and the willingness to continue this training from this point forward, constantly turning your art forever." And he reiterates, "Just because you have bought a security product or three doesn't mean you are safe."

Security products are tools. Like any other tool, they can vastly increase your capability. But still, you must be in control. No tool–whether it is a hammer or an F-16 jet fighter–operates by itself. There is no such thing as an automated process that needs no on-going supervision, any more than a fifth grade teacher can entrust her class to a class monitor.

Make the culture of security your company's frame of reference.

A New York TV news program opens with the slogan, "It's ten o'clock. Do you know where your children are?" Today, in a cyber-environment that spans the world, all time zones and all cultures, it is always ten o'clock. We all want to believe that we live in a zone of safety. That is our personal security, where we can take refuge, relax our tensions and let down our guard. None of us want to be told that wherever we go, we are being monitored by electronic stalkers: that when we are surfing on the Web, someone is recording the sites we visit, someone else is reading the email that we have sent and someone else is establishing control of our computer for possible use in a future distributed denial of service attack.

At work, we wouldn't tolerate an environment where, if we left our office door unlocked, we would find upon our return that it had been ransacked, and that thieves had made keys so that they can break in any time they want. And now that we have extended our domain to that of the Internet, we want to believe that our Internet environment is as safe and reliable as our home and office environment.

In our everyday lives, we entrust our security to the professionals–to the police, the army, security guards–so that we can go about our affairs unencumbered by security concerns. We would like to think that we can do so on the Internet as well–that someone else, or that some piece of software, can act as our police force as we travel on the cyber superhighway.

Even more than that, we have been socialized to believe that people are basically good. We prefer to think that if we are good, then in return other people will reflect goodness back to us. It is a blow to realize that the world is filled with people who have few moral compunctions. We tend to assign rational and even positive motivations to evil people. During the L.A. riots, Rodney King lamented, "Why can't we all learn just to get along?"

But as the Internet exposes us to a wild and untrammeled neighborhood, we find that to look that reality in the face poses a profound and existential challenge to our view of reality.

Thus, changing to a "culture of security" is not only a challenge to our convenience. For many it can be a threat to their ideals. Maintaining such a culture will remain a difficult goal to reach until we can learn how to be protective of our assets without sacrificing the values and ideals that give us our self-respect.

PART TWO

KNOWLEDGE SYSTEMS AND SECURING BUSINESS INTELLIGENCE

CHAPTER FIVE

KNOWLEDGE AS AN ASSET

Overview

There is a direct relationship between cyber-security and an organization's knowledge. Organizations place their crucial knowledge on fragile electronic media and make it accessible to users across the globe through the Internet. There are hordes of blackhats eager to destroy, pervert and misuse that knowledge. Some of them come from without, and others are insiders. As organizations gain a greater awareness of the amount of hostile forces on the one hand and of their data's vulnerability on the other hand, they begin to inculcate a regimen of cyber-security to protect their greatest asset: knowledge.

That is the aspect of knowledge related to security.

However, there is another area in which knowledge can leave an organization. This is the aspect of knowledge related to assets.

When an employee leaves a company, he or she takes along a great deal of tacit knowledge. But this has happened throughout the history of mankind. Why should this be given special attention today? The answer is two-fold.

First, today we live in an era of information. Information is more important than it has ever been before. Raymond Miles, former dean of the Haas School, states, "Many 21st century organizations will succeed or fail in proportion to their ability to manage knowledge, to create and capture know-how, to diffuse it throughout the organization." He estimates that most firms today "make only limited use of the total intellectual capital embodied in their employees. Some organizations may use as little as 20 percent." When a worker leaves with information, he or she is leaving with a very valuable asset.

Secondly, in the last few years, corporations have laid off tens of thousands of employees. In the aftermath of this radical resizing, data has begun to flow in indicating that much of it was unwise and precipitate. Although firing some workers reduced cost in the short run, this policy was short-sighted and poorly-considered. And as a result, many companies that fired workers are doing no better than, and, in many cases, are worse off than those companies that refrained from doing so.

As Mary Bresnahan of the Bresnahan Group writes, "It is no secret that companies that have downsized in order to save dollars often don't achieve their goal (cut costs and make money). Even though their expenses are lowered, they don't make more money as a result. Rather, they are typically in far worse situations three years later than companies who do not downsize.

"According to the U.S. Bureau of Economic Research, manufacturers that downsize are less likely to see productivity gains than those that do not. In a study of manufacturing companies, the 250,000 manufacturers that downsized had an average 4.7 percent return on assets vs. a 34.3 percent return for those that did not."

One reason that these massive layoffs were such a poor idea was that each terminated employee took with him or her a vast amount of tacit knowledge. The corporation may have saved $100,000 a year by firing an individual. But it may take the organization $2,500,000 to recoup the cost of doing do. Peter Drucker remarks, "when knowledge walks out the door, it takes 25 to 35 times that person's salary to replace that knowledge."

Thirdly, the number of employees who will be leaving their jobs in the next ten years–in particular, retiring baby-boomers–will be so significant as to constitute a matter of national urgency, perhaps even international urgency.

How can organizations project themselves against such knowledge losses? They will have to put into place systems that collect and effectively process this information. Those systems come under the general title of *knowledge management*.

Knowledge management will play a crucial role in the years to come, protecting every industry throughout the United States, preserving vital corporate and public sector knowledge so that the United States can remain vibrant and robust.

The Asset of Knowledge

We began this book by referring to September 11 as a crucial turning point in America's culture. The disaster of September 11 was to a great degree a catastrophic failure in knowledge management. In the words of Hamilton Beazley, chairman of the Strategic Leadership Group, "The shocking intelligence failure that made possible the destruction of the World Trade Center was, fundamentally, a knowledge continuity failure–a failure to generate, harvest, interpret, transfer, and preserve intelligence that would have prevented the catastrophe."

Overall, knowledge management accomplishes two things. One, it winnows down an overwhelming amount of data and categorizes it. Two, it makes that knowledge easily and equally available to a broad range of users.

In the aftermath of September 11, it became apparent that amidst the great mass of information that had been gathered about terrorist activity, there existed adequate information to have predicted and stopped that terrorist attack. But the information was lost in a mountain of other data, and only in retrospect did it truly stand out. In addition, fragmentary information was gathered by agencies such as the FBI, CIA and police departments. Often, one piece of information did not seem particularly significant. But when these bits of information were pieced together like a jigsaw puzzle, they became instantly and clearly significant.

Knowledge management would have brought to the fore a great deal of scattered written information, much of it already in reports. Such information, which is part of an organization's database, is called explicit information.

But there is another type of knowledge that is as valuable, although usually more volatile: tacit information–that is to say, information that does not fit into a written model, yet which is crucial to the successful performance of a task.

Such tacit information is important on even the most menial and basic of jobs. For instance, think of an entry-level position such as working in a warehouse of educational materials. The job consists of reading an order form and collecting the material. But even here there is an apprenticeship, a learning curve, consisting of many different little details: where different materials are stored, the cataloguing system, the entire routine from picking up an order form to getting all of the materials ready for mailing.

Even in such a simple, limited environment, there are plenty of exceptions to the rule. For instance, some teaching materials are hard to define, so it is not enough to have a categorizing system to find them–one has to memorize what the categorizer had defined them as. Thus, even this simple job has a significant amount of tacit information, which one learns by being instructed by one's colleagues and employer.

The loss of tacit information due to the loss of an employee can come about through various ways: an employee quitting, being fired, retiring, or remaining with the company but going on to a different assignment within the company.

Whatever the cause, when this happens, "knowledge walks out the door." To quote Hamilton Beazley again, "The loss of knowledge from departing employees poses a threat to the productivity and prosperity of contemporary organizations that is equal to the great business threats of the past century." And America is hemorrhaging from on ongoing loss of employees.

The result of all this is, says Hamilton Beazley, "an appalling scenario of knowledge loss." Today, states Mark Hurd, chief of Teradata (a division of NCR Corp.), "average employee tenure is at an all-time low of 3.6 years. This means that vital corporate knowledge walks out the door every day for good, never to return." In his pungent phrase, employee turnover "sucks knowledge out of companies." *Fortune* Magazine reports that even at the "Best 100 Companies to Work For," annual turnover rates run as high as 24 percent in business services, 17 percent in publishing and 13 percent in finance, insurance and real estate. As for movement within one's company, the annual reallocation rate is more than 40 percent–almost half of all workers in America. Related to this is the fact that many workers are just moving into these jobs, and in need of knowledge. For instance, the Congressional Management Foundation reported in 1999 that close to half of the personal staff of the United States Senate have been in their current jobs for less than a year.

A vivid example of this "knowledge discontinuity" is related by Air Force Colonel Michael Basla, former Joint Task Force Southwest Asia joint communications commander:

> Imagine stepping off a plane in Saudi Arabia knowing that you and only you are in charge of all the U.S. communication systems in Southwest Asia. This alone is a daunting task, yet what made it more daunting was knowing that every 90 days, 99 percent of my personnel

were going to leave my organization and be replaced by new crews. Basically, my people would "high five "each other going in and out the door—that was the continuity I had. It wouldn't have been a big deal if we were digging ditches, but that wasn't the case. We were responsible for providing the commander with sensor information and his command-and-control capabilities. This complex enterprise was critical to the safety of friendly forces and to the accomplishment of the United Nation's "No Fly, No Drive "resolution against Iraq (Basla, 2001).

All of these knowledge discontinuities will grow even more acute in the next five to ten years, when the "babyboomer generation" retires. The "babyboomer generation" refers to the 83 million children who were born in the United States between 1946 and 1964. As they leave the workforce, they will take with them crucial knowledge. For instance, the Bureau of Labor Statistics estimates that 19 percent of babyboomers with executive, administrative, and managerial positions will leave their posts by the year 2008 (20% of the all management positions). But the situation is even more acute than that, because some industries will be disproportionately hit. Some experts state that by 2010 "as many as 60 percent of today's experienced management personnel will retire from the [oil and gas] industry (Clark and Poruban, 2001, p. 74). The Society of Petroleum Engineers estimates that 44 percent of its petroleum engineers will retire within the next seven years (Kornberg and Geattie, 2002, p. 19). As Hamilton Beazley points out, that comes to a total of 321,000 years of cumulative experience. Development Dimensions International reports that over the next few years some companies will experience a loss to retirement of 40 to 50 percent of their executives.

And even that is not the worst of it. The John J. Heidrich Center for workforce Development at Rutgers University found that 76 percent of baby boomers would like to retire before reaching 50 (Working for Fun, 2000, p. A1). Possibly, millions of baby boomers will be retiring early, taking their life-time knowledge with them. But even if this is mitigated by other factors, they may still change jobs—which would, in knowledge terms, have the same effect.

And the same threat hangs over the public sector. By 2005, 71 percent of senior executives working for the federal government will be eligible for employment (Walker, 2001c). The situation is such that Debra

Tomchek, director of human resources management at the Department of Commerce, warns of a coming "crisis at the top." Similarly, the CIO at the Treasury Department warns that the department is "approaching a crisis in information technology skills" because of its "highly experienced workforce, which is moving in great numbers toward retirement eligibility."

As we look at state and local governments, we see the same dynamic. In the next fifteen years, 40 percent of all state and local government employees will become eligible to retire, leading, says a State of Wisconsin Workforce Planning Committee, to "the most significant talent and brain drain ever experienced by government."

The news only gets worse when we turn to look at the Department of Defense. Their attrition by retirement will, in some occupations, reach 50 percent by 2006. Senator George Voinovoich, Chairman of the Senate Subcommittee on Oversight of the Government Management, has written that "the federal work force is in crisis. And nowhere is this erosion more evident, or potentially more dangerous, than in our national security establishment.... If we fail to respond to the formidable human capital challenges in our national security establishment in a thoughtful and deliberate manner, then our best strategies and billion-dollar weapon systems will afford us little protection in an already uncertain future." This is because, as the Secretary of Defense reported in May 2000, that the Department faces a "retirement-driven talent drain" that will bring about "a crisis that can dramatically affect our Nation's ability to provide warfighters with modern weapon systems needed to defend our national interests." In the words of Former Secretary of the Air Force, F. Whitten Peters, the situation is "a time bomb waiting to go off."

Knowledge and the Changing Landscape

As you go through technology magazines and read the current literature, you find an amazing assortment of articles about products and the impressive new companies that develop them: the next killer application, who merged with whom and how various product suites can now address a whole host of corporate ailments. The average reader has to be impressed with technology solutions that can do anything from create instant virtual teams to search for remote subjects across the Web. However, this literature doesn't stress what is really important: the fact that the knowledge requirements of our society are ever-changing and that there is no baseline of need that remains static.

In fact, when you look at the state of the economy, the urgency for personal security and new technology functionalities, you have to stop and think about the fundamental business drivers that have changed in recent years. If your challenge is to predict the future of knowledge management over the next four years, then simply look at how much has changed in the past four years. Four years is the length of time the average college student takes to get a degree, and it is no wonder that students have trouble figuring out what kind of job to prepare for. The real question is, "How do we predict the future of knowledge management when the landscape is changing so rapidly?"

It is important to look at this ever-changing landscape from the perspective of people and society rather than just look at technology products and services. President Bush has identified a major human capital issue in the administration's stated five Priority Initiatives. This policy document points out that over half of the current Federal Government workforce could retire by the end of a second Bush term (2008). By virtue of employee turnover alone, the Bush Administration will preside over one of the biggest changes that have ever occurred in the Federal Government. An example of how the younger, not yet recruited, workforce will change the Federal Government is in the U.S. Forest Service. Older foresters have developed and administered programs that view national forest lands as lumbering operations, oil and gas exploration operations, ranching, etc. Younger foresters are already fighting for these lands to be treated as recreational areas and game reserves, much like large National Parks. What is the list of new technologies required to handle this situation?

Another example is in the Department of Defense. The recent Iraqi War demonstrated a fundamental change in the way wars are being fought. The news media have focused on the "smart bomb" and how that has changed the face of war. But more important is the way that inter-service communication and cooperation have changed. There will always be a need for separate military services, but over the past few years they have been molded into a single fighting force rather than three separate services. This is even more pronounced when you include foreign government fighters being integrated into a single fighting machine. Think about the future needs for instant communication and virtual teams, speech processing technologies, and intelligent systems. Similar fundamental shifts in mission, purpose and technologies are taking place throughout government and industry.

In Peter Ramsaroop's recent book, *Surfing the Leadership Wave*, one critical aspect of this challenge is to accept the fact that change is ever-present and to carefully prepare for the next "wave" of opportunity. As a leader, you must work hard to prepare yourself and your organization for the next wave and then be astute enough to recognize when the right wave comes along. Not all waves are right for you and your organization, but waves of opportunity continue to flow in never-ending repetition. The future of knowledge management is like this. New products and technologies will always appear in the marketplace, but you must be careful to select those that are suitable for you and your organization and then be prepared to put them to use in an effective way.

An important cultural attribute of the American enterprise is this: the degree of personal commitment that an individual is willing to put into a new technology is directly proportional to the amount of personal value that he or she receives. In other words, if we are going to ask employees to change their work habits and use a new set of tools to do their work, then those tools must help them do their work "better" and with as little transitional pain as possible. They must receive personal value that equals or exceeds the effort they must apply to use the new technology. It is probable that far more knowledge management initiatives fail than succeed because the corporation has not taken into account the cultural need for employees to receive personal gain from their efforts. People in other cultures may be willing to sacrifice for the good of the corporation, but not Americans!

An example of how this cultural attribute is affecting today's business environment is the introduction of computer-based training programs. The average employee finds these programs to be highly intrusive. They take time, they take commitment and they take discipline. Such a program can be successful if the employee receives recognition or job advancement, or if having new skills will actually help the worker get more personal job satisfaction. The company must communicate these benefits properly, must offer no-nonsense incentive plans and must otherwise ensure that the employee clearly understands that the pain of taking classes is personally worth it. The company must invest in the infrastructure to make taking classes via the web easy. These "human capital" interventions are as important as any new web-based distance learning technology. Many other examples can be found, from web-based conferencing to participating in virtual team rooms.

There is no question that knowledge management will continue to grow and will someday become as pervasive as today's electrical power grid. In fact, this will happen sooner rather than later. But as the landscape of today's corporate environment changes, knowledge management will change with it.

Many times it is not the employees but the organization that is resistant to change. There are many examples in which technology companies have attempted to create markets through advertising to the end-user but failed to recognize the resistance to change by the corporate culture–not resistance by selected individuals but by the corporations themselves.

This is clearly demonstrated in the use of virtual team-rooms, instant messenger systems, etc. Individual employees would pay dearly for the opportunity to work at home rather than fight commuter traffic. In fact, recent surveys indicate that as many as 37% of all professional employees work at home or out of the office at least one day per week. Why not 75% or 90%? Web-based technologies enable this to occur, but corporate culture resists. Corporations want to see their employees at their desks and feel that employees must work under supervision. This is a matter of trust between the corporation and the employee. Equally important is the trust between the corporation and the supervisor.

What might break the logjam between keeping the traditional corporate commuter-centric business model and the ever-increasing commuter traffic and travel risks in the homeland security environment? Perhaps another 9-11 terrorist attack or SARS-like epidemic will come upon us. Whatever the cause, we know that business drivers will change. And when they change, knowledge management will provide technology solutions. Remember the technology waves that have occurred in the recent past: fax machines, cell phones, email, and the like. There are many more new waves forming. Whether they crest over us or find us riding on top depends on how well we observe and prepare. And whether corporations are willing to accept them.

So, what is the future of knowledge management? It will constantly re-image itself to reflect new business realities. It will continue to evolve into an extension of the corporation with all of us end-users as beneficiaries. More importantly, it will continue to grow as a universal personal productivity tool that extends personal freedom of movement and communication. Why? Because the personal freedom it gives us is greater than the pain of learning new products, overcoming virus attacks, and tolerating slow networks.

Pressure by employees and unforeseen external forces will define new corporate landscapes. This in turn will force corporations to invest further in knowledge The benefits of a highly productive workforce outweigh the pain of organizational change. If you want to look into the future, pay attention to corporations and observe how they adjust to new landscapes.

The Dynamics of Knowledge Management

What issues does an enterprise face when dealing with knowledge and some of the aims and techniques of knowledge management? It should be noted that although knowledge management can be deployed by a software suite such as Knowledge Junction, knowledge management is not computer software, no more than computer security is an anti-virus and firewall software package. Thus, in this discussion of knowledge management, we will refer to various ideas and suggestions that can contribute to knowledge management, and are not necessarily found within a software package.

Mark Hurd, chief of Teradata, states that "Capturing employee knowledge is a new challenge of corporations." And he adds that "employees' intimate knowledge–of customers, suppliers, strategic partners and more–must be captured and catalogued during their tenure. If it is not, corporate turnover could be one of the greatest costs in running a business today."

It should be reiterated that knowledge is different from information. In the words of knowledge management consultant Sheila Campbell, "Knowledge is different from information in that information can be measured in pounds per square inch, millions of instructions per second, terabytes. Knowledge is managing the information to become effective. Information is meaningless unless it can be organized and retrieved in a timely manner and fashion." Tacit knowledge is about judgement as much as it is about facts. Beth Weber of Xerox states that "tacit knowledge is highly personal and includes subjective insights and intuitions based on experience and values."

Knowledge management takes that knowledge–that wisdom, if you will–and gives it to all the members of the enterprise to use and add to. Through knowledge management, information and data are turned into effective action. Knowledge management harvests tacit knowledge so that all members of an enterprise can share ideas. The basic motto of knowledge management may be said to be, "None of us is a smart as all of us."

In addition, knowledge management takes all of the knowledge flowing through the enterprise and makes it easily accessible to all.

One executive tells of his experiences as the co-founder of a startup company, relying on email, the telephone and file-share to manage information. When the business consisted of four members, this sufficed. But once they had two locations–one in the United States and one overseas–and a total of seventy employees, "it was a nightmare to share information and to keep track of the ever-changing direction of the business." They introduced an intranet, which worked for particular processes such as product management and questions and answers. But the only tool they had available to deal with sales and marketing, corporate strategy, competitive intelligence, investor relations and customer management was email.

In retrospect, he says, "If I were to launch another startup, I would deploy a KM solution early on…. With a KM initiative in place at the outset, all the research and information gathered during the business plan creation could be captured in a knowledge base…"

Let us take a look at a number of ways in which information moves through an organization and see what limitations exist in terms of accessing, organizing and saving it. We will refer to this data as "unstructured knowledge." which, in a definition proffered by Unitas Corp., is "information that contains a significant amount of free form text and does not reside in a structured database."

- **Intranet Sites.** Intranet sites can be hard to navigate and can accumulate stale information. When an enterprise has a number of such sites, duplication can occur.
- **Email Messages.** Email contains vital information about many of the enterprise's dynamics and the projects in which it is engaged, but in a fragmentary form, and is often confidential.
- **Groupware Applications.** These include such software programs as Lotus Notes and Microsoft Exchange Public Folders. While these programs have been used effectively to centralize information, that has created its own problem: too much information.
- **Public Web Sites.** These often contain valuable information.
- **Secure extranet sites.** These too often contain valuable information.
- **Word Processing Documents, Spreadsheet and Presentations.** These may be hard to locate or, if stored on a hard disk, susceptible to loss.

- **Multimedia Files and Objects.** These files are often not readily available to all organization members.
- **Discussion Threads.** Similar to email messages.
- **Oral Presentations Transcribed to a Word Processing Program.**

Knowledge management places all of this information in a structured environment, makes it easily searchable and links searches not only to knowledge but to the experts who are creating that knowledge. Peter Drucker states that "the most important achievement of the twentieth century was a fifty-fold increase in the productivity of the manual worker. The most important contribution of management in the twenty-first century will be to increase the productivity of the knowledge worker by a similar amount. [This] is the biggest challenge of developing countries, and will become their only possible source of competitive advantage... On this rests the prosperity of the Western world and the future of its developed economies."

Knowledge management has a broad range of benefits, of which the following are merely a few:

- When knowledge management is implemented, tracking down a piece of information need no longer be a tedious and time-consuming task involving detective skills.
- Many times, hampered in an effort to find a piece of information–or sometimes not even knowing that that information exists–employees "re-invent the wheel." Knowledge management can obviate that.
- When a enterprise can post its most up-to-date information to a centralized information source, it can save even millions of dollars in annual printing costs.
- When an organization is better able to organize sales, marketing and product information, it can better meet the needs of partners and customers.
- When an organization can manage its employee communications, it can supply them with the information they need, keep them in touch with company policies and goals, and provide services such as on-line training.
- Knowledge management makes it possible for employees from a wide range of disciplines benefit from each others' knowledge, and

it makes it possible for employees who have similar knowledge and interests to find each other and work together, by means of electronically mediated consultation and collaboration tools.

Overcoming Hindrances in Instituting Knowledge Management

In order to succeed, knowledge management must have the cooperation of the organization's members. Carrera Consulting, Inc. was a small consulting company delivering ERP solutions to mid-size and large organizations that had to supply its consultants with access to vital information. The need for a centralized, computer-based knowledge bank with up-to-date information was emphasized by the fact that most of Carrera's consultants were on the road. Although Carrera dealt with this well enough in its first few years of operation, as the company grew and employees came and left, Carrera began to face serious knowledge crunches. How could it disseminate the knowledge that had been accumulated and make it available to all employees, particularly the new ones? A central repository for knowledge was created; was to be gathered through sharing and collaboration.

However, the expected sharing and collaboration did not take place. Employees perceived that this system was not in their best interest. Recognizing that much of their value lay in their tacit knowledge, employees weren't ready to make that knowledge freely available. Just as the industrial revolution made craftsmen obsolete, so would a knowledge revolution make knowledge holders obsolete. In addition, the knowledge management system that had been set up required their active participation. They complained that they had neither the time nor energy to work with this system in addition to their already-existing responsibilities.

A couple of lessons can be learned from this case:

- Employees must see benefit to themselves if they are to participate in a knowledge management system. This is not a matter of lecturing them about the ultimate good to the organization. This is a matter of providing that benefit in the form of rewards.

- That system cannot be placed upon the shoulders of employees. Top management must support the knowledge management program and see to it that employees can participate without being burdened.

On the other hand, when a data warehousing corporation called Teradata instituted knowledge management, it took a number of strategic steps to assure employee satisfaction. Among these were the following:

- Teradata teamed up experienced workers with inexperienced workers. The inexperienced workers benefitted from the technical knowledge that the experienced workers possessed. Yet this was to the advantage of the experienced worker as well, for workers were paired off with the goal of placing two people in contact who would enjoy each other's company and find it useful from a social or cultural aspect.
- Teradata promised new and exciting job assignments to its workers. By providing employees challenging assignments, Teradata kept them eager to remain on hand.
- Teradata offered employees retention bonuses and stock options—which, although not as enticing as they had been before the economic bubble burst, are still perceived as a significant bonus.
- Teradata provided development planning—not on a mass level, but on an individualized level.
- Teradata also made sure that job performance standards were clearly defined. This was to avoid what Jerome Colletti, author of *Compensating New Sales Roles*, calls job contamination: "impurities that exist in jobs that cause people to be less than clear about what it is being delivered or what they're getting." When such impurities contaminate a work environment, they create uncertainty and anxiety, leading employees to leave at the first opportunity.

As a result of the above strategies, Teradata staunched an attrition rate that had risen to more than 25 percent. Other things that an employer can do to increase employee morale are:

- Give employees an opportunity to feel that they have some influence.
- Honor employees. Recognize long-term employees if for no other reason than they are long-term, and recognize all employees for their contributions to the company.
- Develop programs that allow employees flexibility and that encourage self-expression and initiative.

And yet another challenge is that effective knowledge management can be a major endeavor requiring commitments of time and effort–commitments that can strain the resources of an enterprise. An article in the November 2002 issue of *TD* magazine states that change does not happen for two reasons: "A belief that if something different is introduced, it will be adopted and take hold. There is no continuing energy put into the change effort until it is institutionalized and a way of life. We typically don't have the stamina and commitment to make things happen. We want immediate results. Keep in mind, however, that you didn't get where you are in business overnight. It was a long, slow process. The same is true of any training effort. You must have a plan as to how you will implement cross training and then follow through to make sure it is happening. Make the necessary adjustments during the process."

Managers can have a tendency to prematurely withdraw from the process of setting up the knowledge management system, with the thought or hope that it is now self-sustaining. Unfortunately, chances are that it is not, and without ongoing managerial support, the system will wither away.

One innovative approach to stemming a loss of knowledge is to treat former employees as alumni. There can be many benefits, both to your organization and to former employees, to maintain a positive, ongoing relationship:

- Former employees can refer job prospects to your company.
- They might one day return to your company with enhanced skills.
- They might refer new business to you.
- They can have positive things to say about you.
- They might come back to serve as short-term contractors or consultants.

Madge Nimocks, director of America's alumni relations for Ernst and Young, states, "We're looking for three main benefits. One is 'boomerangs'–employees that [sic] later come back to us. Another is business development: alumni referring business to us. The third is getting more information about what's going on in the world–having more eyes and ears on the street.... The objective is to maintain lifelong relationships with our employees."

The software to start an alumni network is not inexpensive. One company, SelectMinds, installs a system that starts at $80,000 with ongoing service that costs between $50,000 and $200,000 a year. A competitor, Planet Alumni, charges $7500-$10,000 for installation and a monthly fee that starts at $1,000.

Cem Sertoglu, cofounder of SelectMinds, says that a popular way to gauge the success of an alumni program is to keep statistics on the number of "boomerang" employees. "If you have a rehire rate of 5 percent now, and an alumni network helps you increase it to 15 percent—meaning that 15 percent of everyone you hire has worked for you at some point before–that would save a typical Fortune 500 company about $12.5 million a year in recruiting and training costs."

Another innovative method of retaining knowledge in your enterprise is to cross-train your employees. Because a cross-trained employee can fill several roles, he or she is more likely to remain valuable to the company, along with his or her tacit knowledge and thus will remain longer.

Another difficulty in instituting a knowledge management system is organizing unstructured information.

Information can be in different physical locations, such as personal computers, file servers, email servers, laptops, intranet web servers, and other machines outside of the enterprise. In addition, it is often stored in a variety of formats.

Unstructured documents must be provided with effective metadata.

Much information doesn't exist anywhere in writing, but rather is the knowledge of certain employees. Here is the case knowledge management's tools for collaboration and for making connections between people (not just between people and documents) proves crucial.

Information that is never harvested cannot be passed on to others. Information that is harvested but not winnowed is largely unusable: there is too much of it, it is disorganized and the trivial and meaningful are mixed together so thoroughly that it is hard to tell the difference.

We see a similar problem on the Internet. Do a search for "osteoporosis." What do you do with 500,000 documents that address your topic? How can you tell if what you are reading is an expert's considered evaluation or an enthusiast's unsupported beliefs?

In truth, the answer is already lodged within the question, for a search engine has some of the characteristics of a knowledge management procedure. When you search for a topic on the Internet, you know that the first fifty or a hundred answers are likely to be the most relevant–or, at any rate, they are likely to produce the information that you are seeking. Secondly, information tends to create its own hierarchy. That is to say, you as the reader can often make a reasonable judgement about the believability of information. A site called "The Cure for All Ills is Apple Cider Vinegar" is less likely to have useful information than one called "The Surgeon General's Resource Page." And some pages use grading systems, such as professional reviews and readers' feedback, in order to indicate their worthiness.

Similarly, knowledge management harvests information, organizes it and provides a ranking system of those supplying the information: expert, visitor, and so forth. In the fairytale *Rumpelstiltskin*, the young heroine was faced with the challenge of spinning straw into gold. Knowledge management is very much like that. It gathers huge mounds of information, like straw, and spins them into a meaningful and valuable resource. That resource, which is worth its weight in gold, is knowledge.

When information becomes knowledge, knowledge can become action and innovation. Knowledge management takes away the barriers to the free flow of knowledge. It thus multiplies the value of your company by making available the intellectual capital that it already possesses but has not yet comprehensively utilized. Who wouldn't make an effort to get money out of a bank account that they just discovered lying dormant? Knowledge management is the effort to access the hidden talent and resources within your organization. Use it well, and it will provide excellent benefits for everyone associated with your organization.

CHAPTER SIX

DYNAMICS OF KM: KNOWLEDGE JUNCTIONS

Knowledge: An Open and Shut Case

In order to stay competitive and effective, organizations need to control their knowledge assets. Previous chapters have spoken about securing these assets from abuse and exploitation.

We have also touched on the fact that as we strive to protect our knowledge assets, we must not degrade the quality of that knowledge and its access to authorized users. Any such degradation adversely affects the organization. One can no more run an organization effectively when its knowledge assets are under constraint than one could grow a sunflower that one is keeping in the basement for safe-keeping. In addition, a too-zealous approach to knowledge security runs counter to our shared ideals of democracy and the rights of personal privacy.

There need be no contradiction between greater control of knowledge and greater free flow of knowledge. Knowledge can be secured against unauthorized users and access to it can be made easier and more effective for those who are authorized to use it and add to it.

The Commodity of Knowledge

In bygone days, Calvin Coolidge asserted that "the business of America is business." Today, the business of business is knowledge. For businesses to function effectively, their workers must have instantaneous access to vast amounts of knowledge. But it is not enough for information to be accessible. There must exist an effective means of quickly attaining the specific piece of knowledge that you want.

When Baltimore Hebrew College received funds to update its library, for instance, it chose to install a new electronic catalogue rather than to buy new books. Until that time, the catalog in use did not list all the books that the library owned. The librarian felt that gaining greater access to the material already at hand was superior to gaining more material without improved access.

In all sectors, it is not enough to have access to vast amounts of material. That material must be arranged and catalogued.

An organization's knowledge is composed of its written information and the knowledge of its employees and consultants. The packaging of that knowledge to make it not only available but more immediately useful and to make available not only written knowledge but the knowledge of others is knowledge management.

One such tool of knowledge management is a system developed by EVOLVENT Technologies, Inc., called *Knowledge Junction*^{TM}. In the following pages, we will describe the application of knowledge management, using Knowledge Junction as our paradigm.

Knowledge Junction

Knowledge Junction is an intranet system that is designed to allow people to record and distribute knowledge in a highly effective way. The typical approach to knowledge management is based on the model of the Web, and is largely limited to interfacing with a static environment. Knowledge Junction, on the other hand, allows an employee to interact with the organization more dynamically and powerfully.

Each individual working for an organization sees the organization and its resources from his or her particular point of view. There are as many definitions of the organization as there are people working there. Thus, each individual needs to interact with the organization in his or her own way to be as effective as possible. For example, the knowledge interchange that a salesperson needs when dealing with the organization is different than that which the CEO needs. Each has a different need and each is dealing with a fundamentally different form of knowledge.

Knowledge Junction merges these fundamentally different needs and different forms of knowledge into one integrated system. As a result, people at all levels of the organization can communicate, interact and work together. In other words, while respecting the hierarchical nature of an organization, this system allows and encourages the communication and knowledge-sharing that take place when people at all levels can give and receive from each other.

In by-gone days, political and military leaders would circulate incognito amongst the common people. Today, a factory owner has to go through his plant and see how the equipment is working. So does a leader have to be in touch with what is going on at every level of his or her organization. In order to make the most intelligent and useful decisions, the organization's leaders must have access to the insight and input of lower echelon personnel. Everyone benefits by having open access to each other.

Knowledge Junction can put all organization members in touch with each other. It can take the information that is to be found in every part of the organization and make it accessible to all the members of the organization. Knowledge Junction makes transparent the walls that separate the knowledge contained within every separate unit of the organization. When knowledge from diverse sources is pooled together, new connections are formed, new insights are created and new approaches to challenges can be formulated.

It is Knowledge Junction's purpose to take knowledge from qualitatively different sources in a complex organization and to make it available to a broad range of users. Because this ambitious goal strains the abilities of current web-based techniques, Knowledge Junction uses a new architecture.

Let us say that a manager wants to know how to cut costs. This is a complex question and the best way to answer it is to pool together the expertise, disparate perspectives, concerns and knowledge from every unit within the organization.

One way of speaking about this manager's situation is to say that he wants *soft constructs*. A soft construct is knowledge–but not just knowledge found in a document. It also includes the living knowledge of other members of the organization. Ideally, it is everything that everyone knows, pooled together. In a sense, it is the group culture, the shared body of wisdom and information.

This can be compared to a gathering of an American Indian tribe. Whoever wishes to speak takes hold of a "talking stick" and contributes his knowledge and wisdom, so that knowledge is shared by all. A modern organization is too large and complex to solve its problems by gathering all of its members in an auditorium and allowing everyone to speak.

New technologies must provide the resources that simpler means provided in simpler circumstances. Knowledge Junction is the "talking stick" of the modern enterprise. Knowledge Junction allows intangible knowledge generated by one part of the enterprise to be used by other parts as well.

Knowledge comes in a variety of forms, such as documents, training materials, lists of skilled workers and experts, and collaboration threads. An organization might contain hundreds of sub-units–smaller organizational entities that generate and consume knowledge–and thousands of workers who create the knowledge. In an airline company, for instance, every stratum of the company has its own knowledge and expertise; and within each stratum, there are different viewpoints and areas of knowledge dependent on various locations and variations in the job details. Not only is the knowledge of an airline attendant different from that of an accountant, but the knowledge of an airline attendant on domestic flights is different from that of an attendant on international flights.

An enterprise's intranet may be comprised of hundreds of nodes, each managing hundreds of pieces of information. It is this complexity that Knowledge Junction is designed to address.

Knowledge Junction and Tacit Knowledge

How can we capture and utilize tacit intellectual capital? Knowledge Junction presents a methodology of applying automated tools to generate and capture tacit knowledge–in particular, Knowledge Junction employs two basic tools do so:

- Hierarchical Site Map
- Search and Navigation Tools

Once Knowledge Junction lays out a hierarchical site map, at any point on this map, one may use search and navigation tools. The map and tools are shared equally by all areas within Knowledge Junction.

Hierarchical Site Map

Every large enterprise has clearly identified *centers of excellence* i.e., the major departments within the company that organize and focus individual elements so that there is an integrated and shared goal of attaining the organization's mission. These centers of excellence require support systems that make it possible for them to maintain their operations.

The success of the enterprise as a whole depends upon how well each independent center of excellence is functioning. Each center of excellence has to be able to communicate well with its support systems, and each center of excellence also has to be able to communicate laterally with its peers.

The hierarchical map identifies all of these elements as nodes in a complex labyrinth. In other words, the hierarchical map presents a logical picture of the entire enterprise. Actually, this is a collection of maps–each of which views the enterprise somewhat differently. It is similar to a collection of maps of one area, each map focused on a different aspect: a political map, a geological map, a topological map, and so forth. The hierarchical site map provides a variety of distinct views of the organization with its centers of excellence and their support organizations, in both their organizational and functional aspects.

These multiple views allow users to choose the perspective that best suits their needs. In providing users with this multiple view of the organization, Knowledge Junction helps them enter the flow of knowledge. It helps them determine where to find directories of people, how to utilize communication channels, how to receive training and where to place documents. Once they are there, it helps them participate in that flow–not only taking the knowledge that they need but also contributing pertinent knowledge of their own.

In addition, by creating a flexible and useful configuration, the site map helps manage the sheer volume of knowledge in the enterprise by linking that knowledge to the enterprise's organizational structure.

And so the first layer of Knowledge Junction is a multi-valenced map that organizes the knowledge of a complex entity and then allows that organized knowledge to be viewed from a variety of viewpoints, so that it is available to all units within the entity, and that each unit can use the map to reach other units. By analogy, a hospital could publish a book of maps of its physical structure and the functions carried out in that structure, in order to allow maximum movement and communication between all employees of the hospital. Doctors might have one map that is most helpful to them, and other employees would have maps most pertinent to them.

But these maps would overlap–each map will show the same basic structure–and anyone can look at any map.

Knowledge Junction delineates the forms of knowledge within an enterprise and shows where these areas of knowledge are localized.

Search and Navigation Tools

Although very useful, the Hierarchical Site Map is not yet a sufficiently detailed presentation of the organization and its tacit knowledge. This more detailed presentation is organized in the form of an *index of concepts* i.e., an index of specific terms meaningful to the enterprise. This index compiles all the forms of knowledge that reside in the enterprise.

The Index of Concepts is generally referred to as the enterprise's *taxonomy*. It is organized clearly, and may have as many as five levels of topics and sub-topics. This Index of Concepts is not unique to Knowledge Junction. Such an Index is at the heart of any commercial Internet search engine. It is a powerful tool that allows Knowledge Junction to retrieve appropriate sources of knowledge during any user's search process.

Closely related to the Index of Concepts is a Pointer File. The Pointer File directs the user to every point where a concept occurs within the entire Knowledge Junction map: whether in documents, discussion threads, training materials or any other forms of knowledge. For instance, when a user searches for the term "budget," the Index of Concepts identifies all knowledge that uses that term, and the Pointer File gathers all of these sources and presents them to the user. Now he knows, where any knowledge about the budget exists is any area of the organization, and in what form it exists: as a document, as a department, as a regularly scheduled meeting, as a discussion taking place on an intranet newsgroup, and so forth.

The Four Pillars

All of the areas in the Knowledge Junction are organized into four particular ways that knowledge is recorded, known as "pillars":

- Collaboration Areas
- Expertise Locators
- Document Repository
- Learning Management System.

Let us look at each of these four elements more closely.

Collaboration Areas

Knowledge Junction encourages contact and communication amongst all the members of an organization. Such collaboration can occur in a variety of forms. Basically, we can divide communication into the synchronous and asynchronous. Synchronous communication involves face-to-face conversation, phone conversation and instant messages. Asynchronous communication may be mail, email, written reports and the like. (New and innovative technologies such as the PDA [Personal Digital Assistant] provide true virtual access to anyone at any time.)

Any written form of information, such as email and instant messaging, can be easily added to Knowledge Junction's data base. In addition, speech-to-text technology, which allows users to convert speech into searchable text, makes is possible to transform many heretofore ephemeral modes of communication into recordable knowledge that can be stored and easily retrieved. Thus, conference speeches, briefings, video and audio recordings can be captured, converted into text and placed into tacit knowledge libraries. The same can be done with any conversation captured by a recording device. Thus, the free flow of personal communication, once so fleeting and difficult to capture, can be easily made part of an organization's knowledge base.

It is important not only to capture these topics but also to link them to the contributing individual and to tab them with key words and phrases. Once an audio file has been converted into text, these text files can be scanned by the search engines and made available to users who require that knowledge or contact with knowledgeable individuals.

Broadening the information net does not imply that any individual will be deprived of any measure of privacy. All communications are recorded with the individual's consent, and recordings are limited to topics of broad interest, not to topics involving personal or private concerns. Sometimes the line separating the two may be unclear. For instance, an individual's assessment of some procedure may have the practical consequence of negatively affecting someone else's career. Even if his assessment is cited anonymously, a perceptive reader might be able to determine who he is. Such concerns are not intrinsically different from issues that already exist. The same sensitivities and safeguards utilized until now must continue to be utilized, adapted for the electronic medium.

Participants in the Knowledge Junction must be made aware that their company email communication, remarks at meetings and so forth may be used to enrich the company's data base. Nothing will be used without a member's consent, for the right of privacy and the need for private communication is vital to an organization's health. Organizational members must feel free to express their opinions. When, in October of 2003, a memo by Secretary of Defense Donald Rumsfeld was leaked to the press, it was cited as a document in which Secretary Rumsfeld is questioning the effectiveness of America's military campaign in Iraq. The reaction of those defending Rumsfeld was that he often elicits reactions form his subordinates by making tough statements in order for them to come up with effective stratagems. In a world without privacy, such communication could not take place. Therefore it is vital that the transparency that Knowledge Junction provides take into account the need for appropriate opaqueness in communications between organizational officials.

To return to the area where openness is appropriate and desirable, one important resource for company knowledge is computer-based discussions: message boards and the like. In a large enterprise, one can find literally hundreds of active "discussion threads." A vital function of Knowledge Junction is to record, link and index these discussion threads. The process of following a discussion from one link to another, referred to as *spidering*, is a vital function of Knowledge Junction.

This makes it easy for any user to find and contact an individual involved in such a discussion. Many of the traditional walls that separate figures who possess information and authority have been dissolved by electronic communication. The first barrier that has been dissolved is time, and the second is inconvenience. For instance, if you read a book a few years ago and wished to contact the author, you would have to send him or her a letter in care of the publisher. It might take months for the letter to make its way from the publisher to the author. Then, the author would have to write a letter, find an envelope and address it, stamp it, and drop it in a mailbox. Each inconvenience puts a barrier in the way of open communication.

Nowadays, by contrast, an author will place his or her email address on the book jacket and invite your communication.

Knowledge Junction brings the same open access to an organization. Ordinarily, it may be difficult for a subordinate to catch the attention of a higher-ranking organizational member, but email levels the playing field. The result of open communication is a democratization of an organization as well as an increased meritocracy. It is true that many technologies have raised enthusiasms and expectations unrealistically. Nevertheless, the history of the Internet shows that a complex and robust system of knowledge sharing can enrich and empower people at all levels.

Expertise Locators

One component in the success of Home Depot is the fact that its employees can answer customers' questions about how to get things done. By speaking to a store employee, the customer can describe his situation and receive an appropriate answer. Similarly, sometimes an employee does not need printed information but access to a knowledgeable resource person.

Knowledge Junction categorizes its users as one of four types: experts, contributors, subscribers and visitors.

An **expert** is an individual who is directly and formally identified as such. The owners of the Knowledge Junction (e.g., the chief executives and managers) certify such a person as a **Peer Reviewer**, and he or she has an authorized role in helping others.

A **contributor** is a user of Knowledge Junction who creates shared knowledge by frequently taking part in discussion threads, and by contributing documents to the Knowledge Junction. Although not formally authorized by the organization, such an individual can step forward and earn the status of a resource person.

A **subscriber** is a more passive consumer, someone who monitors Knowledge Junction and takes an interest in new topics, documents, and so forth, but who doesn't contribute knowledge him or herself.

Finally, a **visitor** is a user who needs ad hoc access to the material found on the Knowledge Junction.

Expert	Contributor	Subscriber	Visitor
A Knowledge Junction user with an official role in contributing to the general knowledge data base in helping other individuals	An individual who contributes frequently to the Knowledge Junction database through discussion, written material, etc	A regular user of the Knowledge Conjunction who takes information but contributes little	An occasional visitor to the Knowledge Junction who needs information on an ad hoc basis

A notional metric states that experts constitute less than 1 percent of users, contributors are 1 to 5 percent, subscribers are 5 to 10 percent and consumers are 90 percent.

Creating lists of skills important to the enterprise and associating them with the names of workers who possess the skills is critical in developing the expertise aspect of Knowledge Junction. The full power of the Knowledge Junction is realized only when these lists are assembled and then coordinated with the organization's taxonomy. Then a search in the Index of Key Concepts will yield not only textual documents but also the names of individuals associated with a particular topic.

It is clear how an "expert" or "contributor" will be associated with a particular topic. But how does Knowledge Junction associate subscribers and even visitors? Electronic monitoring devices on the intranet observe the behavior of the individuals who browse the site and record how they participate in its services. On the basis of their participation in collaboration threads, contribution to or accessment of documents, performing searches, and so forth, their names can be associated with particular topics, and the depth of their input can also be evaluated and labeled. The more a person participates, the more interest in the topic and greater skill is imputed to him or her.

Is such a surveillance system is a violation of users' privacy rights? After all, when we go to the library we do not want someone snooping after us and taking note of what books we look up and which pages we read. But before an evaluation of a user is published on the intranet, the user must approve that evaluation. Also, users understand that their work activities are public within the framework of the organization.

Document Repository

How are documents that users contribute integrated into Knowledge Junction?

When information is added to the Knowledge Junction, automated features of the search and navigation system assign identifying labels, or *metadata*, to the document, which identify the type of document and also specify certain Knowledge Junctions. These automated tools are supplied by a commercially available document management system, and apply the principle of Web content management. (The concept is similar to the sharing of large drives throughout an organization–however, this system includes security features, version control and vast storage capacity.)

Every document is scanned and associated with the Index of Key Concepts. This makes it possible for all forms of knowledge to be catalogued and located. And when a user accesses this knowledge, not only is he or she connected as well with the document but he or she can contact the contributor of that document.

Learning Management System

Increasingly, organizations are offering intranet training courses. This too can be incorporated into Knowledge Junction. Such courses are based on so-called *learning objects,* which are short information segments (3 to 10 minutes long), each teaching a single important concept. These learning objects are linked by a Learning Content Management tool in order to form 50 minute learning sessions. And these in turn can be part of a longer training curriculum. Learning objects are searchable, indexed and readily incorporated into search engine technologies.

Knowledge Junction capitalizes on the searchable feature of learning objects in order to treat them as another source of knowledge. Just as the Index of Key Concepts catalogues and locates documents and collaboration threads, so does it incorporate learning objects.

And so when a user searches for some material on a Knowledge Junction, he or she can access the information itself, a list of knowledgeable resource persons or a list of online courses teaching that topic.

In Summation

Even as an enterprise must guard against unauthorized users so must it ensure that authorized users can utilize its knowledge effectively. Knowledge Junction is a powerful tool that makes an organization's knowledge–tacit and explicit–equally available to all members of the organization. This broadened access empowers an organization, for now all users can access the information that they need to learn and can easily connect with other users in order to form partnerships and other useful relationships.

CHAPTER SEVEN

OPTIMAL ACCESSIBILITY

Maintaining Optimal Access

In your desire to protect your organization against the threats from without and within–from worms and viruses, hackers and crackers, con men and swindlers–you can tighten policy so that you attain safety at the cost of your company's well-being. As discussed earlier, this is clearly not an acceptable solution. A farmer needs to protect his grain from mice, but if he locks it up so securely that no one has access to it, the mice will starve, but so will the townspeople.

Securing information in cyberspace cannot be allowed to degrade the ability of authorized users to access and use information. Thus, any discussion of computer security must address not only measures to keep knowledge secure, but measures that allow the free flow of knowledge through the proper channels.

In this chapter we will outline the many ways that your organization can maintain and even enhance robust and flexible information-sharing strategies. When carried out in conjunction with proper security procedures, these methods of information sharing will not threaten your company's safety. It can attain its full strength and vitality, sharing information more freely and keeping that information safe from prying eyes.

When your organization makes sure that its networking systems provide the benefits described below, you can be assured that in addition to attending to security, you are giving your authorized users optimal access to the information and knowledge that they require. Just as computer security concerns can be divided between the technological domain and the human capital domain, so too can we divide the tools to attain optimal access into the technological and human domains.

The Technology Domain

We can sub-divide the technological domain into nine separate categories, each of which deals with products and with the management of knowledge. When these systems are in place, an organization's knowledge is both secure and accessible.

1. Technical Infrastructure

How does data travel through the organization's intranet? It does so through an infrastructure that usually takes the form of a knowledge management system, such as Knowledge Junction. The next issue to address is how that knowledge management system can be secured. We will now list interventions important to maintaining a system that is both open and secure.

The following are important in making the system flexible and easily accessible.

- Universal Directory. A universal directory allows all individuals within the organization to easily locate and communicate with other individuals, bypassing barriers of organizational structure, separate email domains and the like.
- Single Sign-On. Single sign-on means that a user can seamlessly pass from one software program to another, without frustrating delays associated with entering passwords and the like.
- Reliable 24/7 operations. The company must utilize the resources of a professional and reliable hosting organization.
- Telecommunications. Users within the system must have unimpeded access through firewalls, as well as sufficient bandwidth to provide them with a quick response.

2. Content Management

A content management system is a program that gives users the ability to manage large document libraries. The technology for content management is well-developed and there exist several commercial products that will do an adequate job. Make sure that the content management program you use can do the following:

- Document Management. Document management is the ability to fully manage large document repositories. This involves check-in, check-out and version control.
- Document Conversion. The content management program should be able to manage a large variety of document types and to convert them to universal formats such as PDF (Acrobat Reader) "on the fly."
- Records Management. The program should have the ability to manage records through their entire "life cycle."
- Metadata. The program should be able to create metadata, which describes each document. We recommend using a program that uses XML.

3. Search and Navigation

A robust taxonomy combined with advanced search features is very important. Critical features include the following:

- Keyword Searches. This is the ability to search for any word or phrase in any document.
- Thematic Searches. This is the ability to search for concepts or key phrases contained within documents.
- Thesaurus. A thesaurus can provide the user with unique terms, expanded terms, summary terms, acronyms and so forth.
- Web Crawlers. These provide for knowledge discovery at web sites.
- Taxonomy Categorizors. This refers to the ability to check-in documents and fit them into fixed taxonomies and site maps.
- Content Clustering. This refers to the ability to cluster documents into groups of similar meaning.

4. Expertise

Your system should have tools that can assist users in locating people and organizations that can be tapped as resources. Due to the immaturity of this fledgling field, be careful in choosing the products to use. Also, tools must be used within the limits of respecting other's privacy rights and must comply with Homeland Security regulations. The following are some of the most important expertise tools:

- White and Yellow Page Directories.
- Organizational Directories.
- Subject Matter Expert Directories.
- Association. The automatic association of individual skills in the taxonomy.
- Affinity Groups. Creation of "affinity groups" of individuals with similar interests or skills.
- Mining. Mining documents, email and so forth in order to find experienced individuals.

5. Collaboration

Collaboration tools that make it easy for a geographically dispersed workforce to gain cyber-access to the system are critical to the success of any project. Select tools that provide for both synchronous and asynchronous communication. Synchronous communication allows an immediate interchange, and includes such media as instant messaging and virtual meetings. A variety of COTS applications provide such collaboration products. Many of these applications are "boutique" products. Be sure that your system has the following, at a minimum:

- Instant Messaging.
- Email.
- Discussion Threads.
- Team Rooms.

6. Workflow

A smooth and unfettered workflow lies at the heart of the secure and functional system. The following are core workflow features

- Web Content Management Approval.
- Departmental Business Processes.
- Enterprise Business Processes.

7. Institutional Awareness

Institutional awareness refers to providing the user with high-quality resources that he or she could not afford to access otherwise. The following are some specific instances:

- Virtual Library Subscriptions. These provide easily accessible, industry-specific knowledge.
- News Feeds.
- Syndicated Content.
- Bulletin Boards.
- Push/Broadcast.
- "Town Hall" Site. A town hall site opens communication channels amongst geographically-dispersed executives, creating an atmosphere conducive to the free exchange of information.

8. User Profiling

User profiling allows a system to observe the behavior of a user group and then, in order to respond better to those users' needs, modify security policies. User profiling creates a customized work environment to suit specific individuals and groups. It also allows an organization to present various users those aspects of itself that will be most useful to them, based on their job type, location, and currently assigned task. Some factors are the following:

- Personalization.
- User Interface.
- User Profiling.

9. Distance Learning

A Distance Learning program can be transformed to an excellence by integrating learning management systems into a robust collection and content management environment.

The Human Issues Domain

No matter how powerful, technological solutions alone will not provide a supportive environment for your organization's users. Examples abound of companies whose cyber-communication policies failed because they implemented technological solutions without making an equal effort to focus on how individuals do their work. It does not suffice to present users with a sophisticated technological system if they do not know how to use it, are frustrated by it and see no any reason to use it. "Build it and they will come" is an unfortunate implementation plan. Users must be shown how the new system benefits the company and themselves as well, and must be trained how to use it.

Even if your users' cooperation is not complete and not immediate, they and your organization will still experience considerable benefits. For instance, studies have shown that community of practice development must be in place for between six and eighteen months before any fundamental changes in human behavior are attained. Although time is required for change to materialize, once change does occur, it will benefit everyone tremendously.

We all know that a baby will eventually walk and will eventually talk. We instinctively understand that the process takes time–that it is not always linear and that there will be periods of regression. The same applies to the users in your organization. When you put the proper policies into effect, eventually your workforce will adapt and attain the capabilities that the new technology makes possible. The technology itself will not do it.

The following is an outline of seven critical areas in the human issues domain.

1. Communities of Practice

Your business should encourage the formation of communities of practice (COP's). A community of practice is any group of like-minded people working together. It can be a loosely-affiliated "affinity group" of individuals with common needs or interests, or it can be a fully-organized and funded working group. By providing community services to such a group of individuals, your organization will help facilitate collaboration and information-sharing among them. And a group of individuals in a community of practice–individuals who know their specialty well, who know who their colleagues are, who share a common culture and who have an efficient means of communication–are better able to respond to an organization's needs than individuals working on their own, without the common ties of a community of practice.

The following are some important steps that your organization can implement to create such communities of practice:

- Sponsorship. Every affinity group should have its own sponsor. The role of this sponsor is to foster an environment of collaboration and to provide the resources that his or her community needs to sustain itself.
- Identify and Recruit Participants. An outreach program should be instituted, whose job is to attract individuals who wish to join a group that shares their interests or needs. Word-of-mouth can be an excellent mechanism for attracting individuals, however, a more formal outreach intervention can accelerate this process considerably.
- Roles and Responsibilities. Research has identified several key roles that must be filled within formal communities of practice. These roles include that of coaches and facilitators, who sustain activity and maintain content integrity, and of knowledge creators and distributors, who provide members of those communities with knowledge.
- Populate COP. Specific techniques are used (in addition to the outreach group mentioned above) to create and populate communities of practice.
- Message Groups. A collaboration of lists of work groups, affinity groups, and formal communities stimulates collaboration and information-sharing.
- Team Rooms. "Virtual" team rooms that contain documents, lessons learned, discussion threads, and so forth can enhance the performance of instant teams as they react to crises. It allows them to review their behavior so that their behavior in future situations will be significantly improved.
- COP Specific Content. Take steps to enhance the performance of communities of practice so that its members experience increased benefit.
- Integration with COP Specific Applications and Workflow. Members of a community of practice are often involved in informal, repetitive workflow processes. These individuals can be encouraged to carry out those tasks employing more effective standard workflow processes.

- <u>Facilitation Plan.</u> Your organization must develop specific plans whereby these communities of practice will continue to attract participation and will continue to maintain current and useful knowledge.
- <u>Communication Plan.</u> By implementing a specific plan to ensure ongoing communication, your organization will enhance the effectiveness of its communities of practice.

2. Rewards and Incentives

Frequently, project managers lack understanding of the human element. Assuming that monetary compensation is the only means of motivating individuals, they dismiss the need for creative and specific reward and incentive plans. Even worse, they may provide repetitive and meaningless "employee of the month" awards, trite award systems that result in a lackluster workforce.

Enthusiasm cannot be commanded, but must be elicited and nurtured. Lacking enthusiasm, workers will merely do show up and do the minimum. Once they have reached a critical level of ennui, they may even sabotage the organization in a variety of ways, large and small, obvious and subtle. In one company, for instance, a disaffected secretary who had the responsibility of mailing flyers to customers addressed all customers who were physicians as "Mr.," in the hope that they would be insulted and refuse to patronize her boss's products.

At the very least, workers who lack reason to be invested in their company will not lend their energies to creating the knowledge-sharing culture that is necessary for program success. Uncreative incentive systems must be replaced with a carefully thought-out reward plan that features the following:

- Goal Setting
- Individual Incentive Plans
- COP Membership Incentive Plans
- Contributor Incentive Plans
- Corporate Incentive Plans

3. Performance Measures and Metrics

Not all methods of measuring a project's success are equal. For instance, say that fifty people out of a total of sixty possible candidates take a distance learning class. Of these fifty, fifteen utilize the information that they learned and the other thirty-five do not. A person taking a statistical count would report this as a significant success: over eighty percent of the workforce signed up for the class. But a person who measures business effectiveness would rate the program as a failure.

A well-defined program for performance measures and metrics includes the following:

- Establishing Goals
- Defining Quantitative and Qualitative Metrics
- Establishing a Baseline
- Implementing a Metric Collection Process
- Establishing Measurement Standards and Expectations

4. Governance

Your organization must develop specific plans to govern how users will participate in the system. This is especially important when you are attempting to vertically align your company's goals with the goals of individuals and of groups within the company.

These plans must include the following:

- A Governance Model
- Operations Policies
- Content Management Policies
- Technical and Data Policies
- Security Policies
- Architecture Policies

5. Marketing and Communication Plan

Your organization must develop and implement well-designed marketing and communication plan. This must include a training plan for those individuals who will be working directly with the new system.

This marketing and communication plan should include the following:

- Executive Communication Plan
- General Awareness Plan
- User Training Plan
- COP Manager/Roles Training Plan
- COP Recruitment Plan

6. Trust Systems

Frequently, while developing a knowledge-sharing system, people overlook the need to assure the qualifications of the individuals contributing content and maintaining the integrity of that knowledge.

As one example of questionable knowledge, when it was discovered that Nancy Reagan was employing astrologers and based on their prognostications she might have been influencing President Reagan's executive decisions, there was an uproar, because most people do not feel that astrologers are individuals qualified to give reliable geopolitical information. Your organization must provide the framework that will make sure that only qualified personnel and reliable data form the knowledge base of your communities of practice.

7. Subject Matter Expert (SME) Development

In many organizations, barriers have been set up that prevent knowledgeable individuals from becoming visible to the knowledge-sharing community. What is the nature of those barriers? Basically, they can be one of two, and often consist of a combination of both these factors. The first factor is personality. The person in charge blocks access to a person on a lower echelon, because the person in charge does not appreciate what the person on a lower echelon can offer, or he may feel threatened by him. Secondly, the hierarchical nature of the system may make it difficult for a person on the bottom to be heard.

At any rate, many present-day organizations have the unfortunate characteristic of stifling the voices of the people at the bottom. In the military, for instance, the chain of command and rank frequently prevents junior officers or senior enlisted men from contributing their know-how.

It is important that policy-makers institute a culture and policy that will encourage the participation of all individuals in the organization, that will give them all the sense that their participation is welcomed and valuable, and that will make all knowledgeable individuals and their know-how visible to the knowledge-sharing community.

The Gold Rush

A prospector who is panning for gold has a dilemma. If his sieve's holes are too small, he will have to process too much silt. If its holes are too large, gold nuggets will fall through with the worthless silt. So the gold prospector has to make a reasonable accommodation. He uses a sieve that may not capture every sliver of gold, but on the other hand he won't waste time and energy digging through sand.

Knowledge management is like the sieve, and the gold is the knowledge that you want to access. Constrict the flow of knowledge too much and no useful process will take place. Open it too much and your gold will flow away and be lost. The correct use of knowledge management assures you that your prospecting will yield profitable results for you, and will keep the gold away from rivals.

Fortunately, there is no need to buy a burro and prospecting equipment and head for the hills of California or the Sierra Madre. The gold in your organization is right now waiting to be sifted and gathered.

When you put in place a knowledge management system that addresses the nine dimensions of the technology domain and the seven dimensions of the human capital domain, your organization will reach the goal of optimal accessibility. Knowledge management is a proven methodology with powerful results. When you make use of this tremendous resource, your organization will grow more robust, resilient, energetic and dynamic.

CHAPTER EIGHT

PROTECTING THE HUMAN CAPITAL

Human Capital: Our Greatest Asset

Human capital can be defined as the knowledge, skills, competencies and attributes embodied in individuals that facilitate the creation of economic, social and personal well-being. Human capital is perhaps the single most vital factor in today's knowledge-based economy. More than any other single factor, it determines levels of output. The competitiveness of a firm or of an entire country is determined by its human capital. If ten thousand clerks were to emigrate from America, it would have little effect. But if ten thousand creative thinkers were to leave the United States, the effect would be dramatic.

Technology cannot substitute for human capital. Although the modern computer has fascinating capabilities, the human brain remains the most powerful supercomputer ever created. Thus, many businesses and organizations frankly acknowledge that their organization's greatest asset is its human capital.

As knowledge grows increasingly important, other resources fade in comparison. The difference in success between Xerox and IBM, the difference between Coca Cola and Canada Dry increasingly rests upon a difference in the quality of human capital and the way in which it is utilized.

Thus, every organization must strive to develop its own human capital and at the same time protect that capital from hostile attack.

As technology spreads, the ability to work with technology becomes increasingly urgent. Hundreds of years ago, intellectual knowledge capital was relatively unimportant. Leonardo da Vinci has left us drawings of a projected helicopter. But these remained drawings. The technology in his day could not meet the challenge of actually creating what da Vinci dreamed of. In his day, intellectual capital took a back seat to brute force of numbers. Today an enterprise's most valuable capital is its knowledge.

Our Knowledge-based Workforce

The real significance of technology upon human capital can be seen in the fact that in our economy as a whole, almost any job requires computer skills of one type of another, and a knowledge of a variety of cyber-tools.

Our knowledge-based society requires not only the facility to use technology, but the capability to adapt to new developments as well. Therefore, lifelong learning is essential. Some of the tools to attain that continuous or lifelong learning are provided by the knowledge society itself: tools such as e-learning, on-line or with CD-ROMs, can be a major component in improving one's skills or adapting to new tasks, technologies and techniques in the workplace and in society at large.

Although it is to be expected that schools and universities will provide a sound basis in the technology of knowledge, that cannot be enough. Companies providing employment must devote an important part of their resources to ensure that employees are able to work with the most recent technological and organizational developments. Today, that investment is as necessary as physical equipment.

However, companies may be reluctant to invest in human capital, since employees trained at significant expense may leave for another job after a brief period of time. It may become the role of government to provide such training. Alternatively, an ideal vehicle for providing the funds for training might be a public-private partnership.

However it is done, such training is most efficacious when it provides workers with new roles and tasks, and involves them in significant organizational changes, consulting with them and giving them appropriate technical training. Surveys show that in response to such measures, workers' performance improves markedly.

Human Capital and Security Issues

When bandits waited alongside the road for a stagecoach carrying a chest full of coins to the local bank, they weren't displaying any acumen about the banking system and its national and international networks. It was enough for them to know that the money was passing this point.

Today, cyber-criminals may have as little understanding about the uses and reasons for the importance of human capital–yet this makes them no less effective in their attempts to attack that capital.

Our knowledge technology needs a substantial number of people with the know-how and skills to protect knowledge. Increasingly, what concerns organizations is not the misappropriation of physical goods as much as it is the misappropriation of knowledge. Thus, as our civilization enters a new phase, it must develop increasingly sophisticated means to protect their new and often intangible asset.

As more knowledge is accumulated, and the means of recording that knowledge grow more sophisticated, several things happen:

- Knowledge becomes easier to steal, counterfeit and alter.
- Knowledge becomes more ephemeral, as electronic media are less stable than traditional records, such as printed material.
- The ability to save knowledge in multiple locations in order to keep it safe becomes increasingly easy. What once would have required an entire library to hold can now be stored on a few CDS.
- New methods of protecting data, such as encryption, are constantly being developed.

In brief, the present picture of the security of human capital is mixed. Like all other innovations, the cyber-revolution is not mono-cultural. It does not only strengthen or weaken what already exists: it completely transforms it.

Every revolutionary change in technology is at first used merely as a crutch to expedite already-existing technology. Only as time passes do its many ramifications make themselves clear. For instance, when Alexander Bell invented the telephone, he saw it as a device whereby a person could call another to tell him that a telegram was on the way.

The same holds for our new ability to access and share human capital. In the dynamics that develop over the coming years, the new shape of this computer-assisted access to human capital, in some ways fragile and in other ways tough and resilient, will take on greater clarity. The actions that we take today to develop our utilization of human capital and the security of human capital will determine its lineaments in the years to come.

Our Changing Knowledge-Society

The knowledge society is characterized by change. Old structures associated with the industrial economy are being transformed. But even the newer structures rapidly grow outdated. The computer miracles of twenty years ago now seem quaint and antiquated. The 5 1/4" floppy disk seems as distant as the buggy whip, and no one can imagine going back to a world where computer monitors only displayed green letters on a black screen and the concept of the Internet was sheer science fiction. The personal computer was originally seen as a more effective and sophisticated typewriter. The idea that a computer could also be a telephone, a CD player, a music studio, a teaching device and an instantaneous portal to literally millions of sites from Alaska to Zimbabwe was beyond imagination.

Even as the newest technology is constantly being transformed, the knowledge economy needs to become more flexible as it reacts to faster technological development. This can be difficult, for the pace of development is so rapid that we cannot adequately integrate changes and comprehend them. This makes it difficult to appreciate both the opportunities and the dangers. We can grow overwhelmed by change, and not know what our decisions portend. There is too much information for us to absorb (a plethora of "junk" information that is either irrelevant or misleading, and a slew of vendors persuading us that they have to offer the real McCoy), or too little information that we can understand. We are entering a new world whose outlines we cannot yet see. The only thing certain is that this world will bring with it many changes and demand many accommodations–many of them unforeseeable.

As access to human capital grows more robust, workers may feel less secure. They may feel that the information they have gathered over many years of work–skills, knowledge, databases, access to expert individuals–helps guarantee their usefulness and thus their security. To many workers, freer access to human capital may be very threatening.

And whereas new tools can make workers much more effective, they also require workers to retrain and, like many other new technologies that have transformed society, they may make workers obsolete. Rather than lead to increased openness and cooperation, an incompetent approach to knowledge management may lead to worker alienation and distrust. In an over-flexible economy, social capital is at risk. These factors must be recognized and dealt with. For instance, social dialogue, either directly between employers and workers (capital and labor) or involving public authorities as well, can help counteract such problems as lack of trust.

The use of the Internet itself has brought with it unexpected issues and complications. Predictably, the rosiest prognostications of the Internet enthusiasts failed to recognize that human nature cannot be changed by technology, but that human nature remakes technology in its own image. Radio, television and the Internet were originally touted as technologies that would transform society by providing knowledge and culture. Doubtless, the Howard Stern radio show, Jerry Springer television show and pornographic web sites are not what these enthusiasts had in mind.

Even beyond the content of these new media, their very form changes us in ways that we could not have predicted. "The medium is the message," Marshall McLuhan stated. The Internet, which was to have been used as a tool of interaction, turns out also to have an unexcepted side-effect: the more time that people spend on the Internet, the less contact they have with their social environment (up to 15 percent of people spending more than 10 hours a week on the Internet report a decrease in social activities). New forms of relationship and semi-relationship come into being, utilizing chat rooms and message boards.

In brief, the developments that offer us the jewels of human capital also disclose dragons guarding those jewels. It is the role of responsible policy makers to study these situations as they unfold and take pro-active steps to help maintain a positive culture, high cohesion and smoothly-functioning social networks.

And it is the role of leaders to identify the security implications of knowledge systems and then take measured interventions. The abuse of human capital can involve anything from hacking a file to blowing up a computer center. The protection of human capital is a critical component of a nation's responsibilities. Thus, the struggle against such destruction must be equally many-faceted, and must involve the efforts of all levels of society, from private industry to the public sector.

PART THREE

CASE STUDIES

CHAPTER NINE

CASE STUDY
LEADERS IN KNOWLEDGE MANAGEMENT

Knowledge Management

Knowledge management is one of your company's most valuable assets, the means whereby the knowledge of your employees can be shared in order to help the organization meet its goals. Access to this knowledge is so important that Harvard Business Review has identified it as the information economy's essential source of competitive advantage. And because this information is one of your company's most valuable assets, it is essential that your company secure that knowledge.

In this chapter, we will turn our attention to how two major organizations–the World Bank and the United States Air Force–lead their respective sectors in utilizing the tools of knowledge management.

In the public sector, World Bank, one of the world's largest sources of development assistance, uses its financial resources, staff and extensive knowledge to guide developing countries onto paths of stable, sustainable and equitable growth. World Bank is also highly involved in knowledge-sharing initiatives for companies and governments worldwide. As such (as well as in its own organization), World Bank has demonstrated award-winning initiatives in knowledge management and knowledge sharing.

In the federal sector, we will look at the United States Air Force Medical Service. This agency faced the challenge of managing health care data from many different locations around the world. Because many systems were operating on different levels, managing patient data and outcomes and other critical data became overwhelmingly difficult. The Air Force's needs were answered by Knowledge Junction, the improved architectural design for knowledge that was introduced in Chapter six.

World Bank

The World Bank, one of the world's largest sources of development assistance, is an international organization whose knowledge derives from the intellect and experiences of a staff of 10,000, as well as clients and developmental partners. This wealth of knowledge must be available as a resource for employees across the globe, as well as other interested parties: for anyone, in or out of the organization, who wishes to find information regarding development challenges. As noted in various publications and websites, the World Bank is an acknowledged benchmark case study in the utilization of knowledge management practices. This representation reflects a synopsis of publicly available information.

In 1996, after World Bank President Jim Wolfensohn articulated a vision for a Knowledge Bank, World Bank began its Knowledge Management initiative. The World Bank Institute, which is the World Bank's knowledge, learning and capacity-building arm, instituted a project which it called Knowledge Sharing.

In March, 1997, the bank's Executive Board voted unanimously in favor of instituting an action program called the Strategic Compact. The purpose of the Compact was to lower the bank's costs, raise productivity and improve the quality of the projects and programs it supports. The basis of its technique would be knowledge management. The Compact states, "The knowledge management system will provide a corporate memory of information, lessons learned from experience, and best practices, but it will also incorporate the best development knowledge from other organizations."

Web Availability

This knowledge bank is presently available online. In this centralized location, one can find programs providing knowledge about the bank as well as connections to many knowledge-sharing communities.

In addition, the bank provides an internal site that facilitates communication amongst its employees. This site incorporates all of the features of the public site and adds more proprietary information, such as meeting minutes or working documents. This site also provides a corporate directory, which manages human resource documents.

Allocation of Resources

Bruno Laporte, manager of the World Bank's Knowledge Learning Services, explains that the bank follows a highly decentralized process for the allocation of resources to knowledge management initiatives.

According to Laporte, knowledge sharing is often held within the framework of "thematic groups" (another name for communities of practice). These thematic groups are the heart and soul of knowledge-sharing at the bank. There are more than a hundred such groups, which reflect a diverse membership and bring an enormous amount of expertise with them, which they then apply to various areas.

Each thematic group contains an advisory service that addresses questions and serves as a focal point for information about any particular subject.

Across the globe, many regional knowledge management programs are active. These programs have a variety of initiatives. In addition, they sponsor other programs. For instance, a KM program utilizes a knowledge portal based in a particular country that provides news, information and knowledge. The bank has an extensive collection of economic and social statistics and indicators, and these are gathered in the regional thematic group. The bank also maintains a "set of best practices" for the work that is carried out in a specific region. Finally, the bank provides debriefing programs, the purpose of which is to help thematic groups share the tacit knowledge that they have gained in the course of their experiences. Indigenous knowledge programs record the indigenous practices in specific countries and various regions within each country.

All of this information–referred to internally as knowledge nuggets–is catalogued in a warehouse system for storing and retrieving information that is referred to as the bank's Business Warehouse. Once the information is there, communities of practice can extract knowledge as they wish.

In order to help users, the bank provides a range of tools, which include interactive websites, online discussion and video conferencing, making use of the distance-learning centers under the aegis of the Global Development Learning Network (GDLN).

The bank is presently in the process of adopting a content management system based on Vignette software. Vignette, a software suite that is also used in many other organizations, primarily in the private sector, makes the process of updating and adding information much easier. Little technical proficiency is needed, so that someone inputting the changes does not need to know how to code or use a program (such as Dreamweaver). The bank's goal in this regard is to democratize the process of inputting and managing content.

Although the bank's knowledge agenda began primarily as an internally focused process, it is growing increasingly externally focused, and is concerned with capacity building.

The World Bank divides its knowledge management agenda into three areas:

- The sharing of knowledge in order to improve the banks' internal effectiveness, i.e., the effectiveness of the staff and the quality of the bank's products and services.
- The sharing of knowledge with clients and partners through a few agencies: the bank's external website, the Global Distance Learning Network (GDLN), the Global Development Gateway, and other global knowledge initiatives. Because the knowledge in these facilities can flow in two directions, the bank can share its knowledge and learn from its clients as well.
- The building up of the knowledge capacity of bank clients, which makes it possible for them to make better development decisions.

Through constant learning from other corporations, the bank is "learning by doing." In the process, its knowledge management system is evolving very rapidly. Its key inspiration has been its constant interchange and benchmarking with outside corporations and organizations such as the American Productivity and Quality Center and IKO (IBM's Institute of Knowledge-based Organizations). The bank draws upon the best innovation across industries to make progress, and is often seen as a source of inspiration in the field of knowledge management for other organizations.

Citing the slogan that "knowledge is the currency," Bruno Laporte explains, "KM is part of our overall strategy. Especially after 1996, it's become apparent to everybody within the bank that KM is part of our business. KM makes our job better and makes the outcomes better. It is connected directly to the overall strategic vision for what the bank is doing."

The bank continuously monitors its knowledge management to measure its impact. For instance, the bank takes note of how much is being spent on knowledge management, the number of programs involved, and so forth. Then the bank looks at what innovations are taking place within the knowledge management system: best practices, new tools, "knowledge nuggets," added resources, processes and so forth. Finally, the bank takes note of how extensively the system is being used: the number of visitors to a website, the number of queries to attain information and the number of requests for help from advisory services. In addition to collecting this data, the bank also conducts internal client surveys.

Staff are also questioned as to the extent to which people feel they have access to knowledge to do their work and the extent to which global knowledge is perceived to be available to clients. Some external surveys conducted in the African region asked about the improvement in access to knowledge through the bank and the extent to which the bank is doing a good job at adapting global knowledge to local conditions.

Laporte notes that the largest obstacle to the successful implementation of this knowledge management system is the amount of time it takes for the culture of an organization to change. He cites, in particular, "trying to get people to recognize the value of sharing knowledge and learning form each other within the organization; asking questions when they don't know something, and sharing what they do know; looking at the accumulated knowledge, and recognizing the value of the free flow of knowledge within the organization."

Laporte says that the bank is addressing these issues in a number of ways. The bank is changing formal evaluation systems, instituting recognition and award programs, providing knowledge fairs, and inspiring teams to improve their behavior through the use of inspiring stories, and raising people's awareness as to how knowledge management is beneficial.

Laporte takes the long view, noting that "this is an on-going task–it takes more than five years to change the behavior of an entire organization." However, he notes, he has already seen significant changes. The bank has shifted from being an inward-looking institution to opening up and sharing more of what it knows with external partners.

One program, the Development Marketplace, began in 1998 with the goal of funding development projects that might otherwise not have gotten off the ground. The Development Marketplace continues to provide startup funds to a diverse group of civil society, public sector and private sector groups launching new and innovative projects in areas such as health, tourism, education, environment and commerce. This concept of an open marketplace matching good ideas with resources has spread to various countries, so that today development marketplaces exist in Brazil, Thailand, Guatemala and other countries.

Here we see how a sprawling, international organization, which deals with many indigenous cultures, whose workforce speaks many different languages and comes from many different backgrounds, and which is involved in dealing with many different economic, cultural, social and religious groups is using the principles and tools of knowledge management to make its knowledge, explicit and tacit, available to all members of the bank, as well as to those outside the bank. As Laporte states, such a project, which is so large and which requires shifts in focus, attitude and awareness of those involved, does not take place overnight, nor does it unfold perfectly according to a master plan. As the knowledge management system is put into place, there will be points of friction and areas where revisions must be made. Nevertheless, although the World Bank's institution of knowledge management is a work in progress, the Bank has already derived benefits from this program and provided benefit to others.

Unlike a static body of knowledge, knowledge management is in continuous flux and growth, and like any other on-going, process-based system, knowledge management will take unexpected turns, developing or ceasing to develop in unexpected ways. Thus, even after such a system is put in place, it must be continuously monitored.

When an enormous body of knowledge is flowing into a knowledge management system, one of the most important tools is not gathering that knowledge, nor categorizing it but winnowing it down. Knowledge can quickly grow stale. What does one do with last month's statistics? There are no perfect answers. Rather, decisions are made taking into account the organization's limitations (such as monetary constraints) and its most important goals.

The Next Level
Knowledge Junctions and Air Force Medical Systems

The Air Force Medical Service (AFMS) provides care to millions of active duty personnel and their families in more than 75 facilities around the world. An integral part of the Military Health System, the AFMS provides peacetime care and assures the delivery of expeditionary medicine as required by the operational commitments of the Air Force in times of war or any military action. An integrated health care delivery system in all respects, the AFMS is responsible for the overall wellness of active duty personnel and clinical facility operations, and it maintains medical readiness to support Air Force missions. Operating in all major theaters and delivering a broad range of health care services, the AFMS faces an incredible knowledge challenge.

Additionally, the military requirement to rotate personnel to different duty stations and different positions means that the AFMS has a constant staff turnover of all active duty personnel. Also, government recruiting difficulties have created chronic shortages in personnel and training. Broader health care sector difficulties in certain specialty areas are even more acute in the Military Health System.

Thus, both clinical and non-clinical staff in the AFMS face an overwhelming challenge of meeting the mission requirements of both peacetime and wartime in an environment of high staff turnover and limited systems capability.

As in many large organizations with distributed operations, the appeal of web technologies was not lost on the AFMS. From 1996 and onward, Web sites and competing local entities and corporate level intranets proliferated. By 2002, over 1,000 sites were in operation containing large amounts of knowledge, much of it duplicated, with little or no control over content and containing a great deal of out-of-date material.

Both corporate staff and regional headquarters decision-makers made several product investments. Some very useful web sites were built and hosted in a "hobby-shop" fashion. Even some complex projects involving large numbers of end users were started to help alleviate the knowledge challenge. In 1999, an enterprise "Knowledge Center" was started. The Knowledge Center initially served to allow geographically disparate groups to share information, post briefings, and start discussion groups. But due to a variety of "human factor" issues, the Knowledge Center was only a limited success.

Also in 1999, following industry best practices, the AFMS consolidated subscriptions to medical journals and created a Virtual Library. This professional clinical content is of enormous benefit to the field clinician and has been a major KM success story to date with millions of data retrievals each year.

By the beginning of 2003, over 60 individually funded and fundamentally diverse web sites proliferated in this Knowledge Center and over 400 other web-sites contained a variety of "knowledge nuggets." To deal with this, AFMS's Chief Knowledge Officer, Lt. Colonel Detlev Smaltz, and

Deputy Major Matt Escher, took on the mission of creating a "Web-based knowledge sharing network and a knowledge repository" for the AFMS, whose goal is to facilitate the ability of the greater Air Force medical community worldwide to communicate freely and access intellectual capital: this is known as the AFMS Knowledge Exchange.

Within the Knowledge Exchange, a new architectural design called Knowledge Junction™, a proprietary application of EVOLVENT, was implemented. As was previously discussed in Chapter six, the working tenet of Knowledge Junction is the merging of fundamental forms of knowledge via a large enterprise intranet. This approach recognizes that the "working part" of an organization varies for each service member and provider. There are as many needs as there are users of the system. The knowledge in Knowledge Junction is made available to these users in the form that is most helpful to them, thus going beyond the traditional model of a static, shared document repository. Users' searches for knowledge are often extensive, often seeking out and finding relevant material that in earlier days might have been inaccessible, because it had been stored in divergent parts of the AFMS enterprise by unrelated personnel.

Knowledge Junction was implemented within the Knowledge Exchange in order to create and distribute knowledge from qualitatively different sources, making meaningful knowledge available to a broad range of users in the complex AFMS organization. The Knowledge Exchange also consolidates Web sites, eliminates out-dated and voluminous documents found in multiple shared drives, facilitates access to subject matter experts and creates online project workplaces.

Utilizing lessons learned from previous AFMS efforts, the Knowledge Exchange builds on the principle of distributed web content management, employing the average end user basic desktop computing skills as the baseline for input and maintenance of content. This is a cost and utility principle, based on the concept that no effective KM strategy can rely on a central organization for its implementation and maintenance. All users must be able to easily access, input, update and utilize the information found in the Knowledge Exchange.

Implementation Model

Critical to the implementation of the Knowledge Exchange is the integration of both the technology and human capital domains (as will be listed below). As the AFMS moves forward with the Knowledge Exchange, a total of seventeen features will be developed. Each of these dimensions is treated as a separate and semi-independent area with its own component model, intervention list, skill set and implementation schedule. Thus, any given dimension can approach 100 percent completion independent of other dimensions. one hundred percent completion of all seventeen dimensions is not necessary in order to harvest benefits from the Knowledge Discovery and Knowledge Sharing system. By analogy, an athlete does not have to develop all of his muscles equally in order to excel, but he is required to develop all of them to at least some degree. In the manner of a continual vector check, a constant evaluation of return on investment and the practical value of the Knowledge Exchange for the AFMS mission means that operational needs of the AFMS will dictate the timing of each component of the model's implementation.

This phased implementation model allows the AFMS to be flexible in implementing the program so as to conform to changing priorities and volatile funding streams over multiple budget years. This model also takes into account the fact that some of its proposed functions are relatively immature and still heavily dependent on factors such as research and development, venture capital-funded startup companies, and newly-released products.

Major Technology domains of the Knowledge Exchange Content Management

The AFMS Knowledge Exchange (KX) utilizes EVOLVENT's Knowledge Junction integrated with Stellent, a commercial content management system. Given high ratings by Gartner Group analysts, Stellent has the ability to manage large document libraries as well as the content displayed on web sites contained within the KX. This content management functionality allows multiple file types to be stored in the document repository. It also possesses version control, security and other standard features. Its key capability is the ability to rapidly create distributed web content nodes on the KX without the need for sophisticated technical skill sets. In the first six months, over 10,000 users have registered for KX accounts, which have driven the activity level to more than 100 times that of previous initiatives in the AFMS.

Search and Navigation

As important as the ease of creating and maintaining content is the ability to readily retrieve that knowledge. The discipline known as "Knowledge Discovery" requires a robust taxonomy combined with advanced search features, among which the following elements are critical:

- Keyword Searches. The ability to search for any word or phrase in a document.
- Thematic Searches. The ability to search for concepts or key phrases contained within documents.
- Thesaurus. Unique terms, expanded terms, summary terms, acronyms, and so forth, are to be found in the search engine thesaurus.
- Web Crawlers. These provide for knowledge discovery at web sites both in and outside of the organization.
- Taxonomy Categorizers. These have the ability to check-in documents and place them in fixed taxonomies and site maps.
- Content Clustering. This makes it possible to cluster documents into groups with related content.

The KX utilizes many of the above features to allow end-users to easily access the body of knowledge available in a manner most intuitive to the individual's working style.

Technical Infrastructure

As it evolves, the KX is being fully deployed within an Enterprise Architecture framework that is consistent with industry standards and other Air Force initiatives. Several major Air Force projects are underway which will provide potential solutions to the following thorny technical infrastructure elements that will be critical priorities in the next phases of development:

- Universal Directory. This allows all individuals to locate and communicate with other individuals irrespective of the formal channels represented by organizational structure, email domains and the like.
- Single Sign-On. This enables users to seamlessly pass from one commercial-off-the-shelf (COTS) product to another without frustrating delays associated with entering passwords and re-authentication.

- Telecommunications. This provides secure access through firewalls as well as sufficient bandwidth in order to provide for quick user response.

Content Channels

The KX enables the development of sophisticated Content Channels, which supply the user with a high-quality work environment. Through Content Channels, the organization gives the individual user tools and sources of information that it would not be financially feasible for an individual to access. For instance, the organization can subscribe to syndicated content and industry-specific virtual libraries, and it can maintain a "best of breed" list of valuable external links. The AFMS Virtual Library is a component of the KX. Coupled with many other previously described features of the KX, it provides a content-rich KM application for clinical and non-clinical users.

Broadcast technologies built on the conceptual element of Institutional Awareness can open communication channels between all users and executives by providing a Town Hall atmosphere, where a free exchange of information takes place amongst members of a geographically dispersed workforce. Leadership briefings, executive retreats, etc. are all examples of how this is being utilized in the KX.

Expertise

Expertise systems, or Knowledge Discovery tools that search out "who knows what," are presently still in their infancy, and due to the immaturity of the marketplace, product selection and implementation approaches must be carefully managed. In addition, consideration must be given to protecting individual privacy and complying with federal and corporate regulations. The following starting points are important functions of this dimension:

- White and Yellow Page directions.
- Organizational directories.
- Subject matter expert directories.
- Automatic association of individual skills with taxonomy.
- Creation of "affinity groups" of individuals with similar interests or skills.
- Mining of documents, email, etc. for the purpose of discovering individuals with specific knowledge and skills.

It is also vital to maintain the KM vision in alignment with organizational priorities for the declaration and definition of expertise.

Collaboration

Collaboration tools that allow a geographically dispersed workforce access to the system have been critical to the success of the KX. Tools must be selected that allow both synchronous and asynchronous communication. A variety of COTS products that meet specific Air Force security requirements can be chosen for this purpose. "Boutique" products proliferate. At the very least, the core collaboration technologies are as follows:

- Instant Messaging
- Email
- Discussion threads
- Team rooms

Further enhancements are planned for greater email and messaging integration with the KX. One popular feature thus far has been that of allowing users to subscribe to particular content elements or Knowledge Junctions. This enables distributed working groups to maintain visibility of updates and changes.

Organizational Learning

The KX allows users to access learning modules online, as well as to communicate directly with facilitators and experts and to access highly relevant content. Furthermore, the KX can offer its own quality learning modules, transcripts, complete course curricula and the means of tracking individuals' learning process, resulting in a better-trained and more focused workforce.

Conceptual Clarity
The AFMS Knowledge Exchange and Human Capital Domains

Implementation of technology will not in itself solve all of an organization's business problems. Many examples of projects exist that were foiled because they over-emphasized the technology solution, neglecting a proper focus on how individuals do their work and how organizations can best modify their behavior to make use of technology tools. Thus, the AFMS KX project team paid close attention to the Human Capital issues inherent to the organization such as staff turnover and rotations and the distributed nature of operations.

Many aspects of human behavior are not susceptible to rapid change. When approaching the problem of sharing knowledge across the AFMS, it became very clear to the project team that this was going to require a long-term, sophisticated implementation effort to really make a major impact on the organization. The development of communities of practice is becoming critical in the AFMS, as these groups act as "change agents" for the enterprise as a whole. Whether it is a specific area of clinicians or a support service function, the growth of Knowledge Junctions has highlighted that the organization can change behavior and knowledge can be shared. In spite of the fact that a period of time is required for many dimensions to materialize, the benefits of a long-term strategy result in highly beneficial results at every step of the way.

Several key Human Capital issues addressed by the AFMS KX team are highlighted below.

Governance

A true enterprise version of the KX cuts across many inter-organizational boundaries. The senior level commitment to the KX has been extraordinary and has really allowed the AFMS to move forward quickly to consolidate resources and allow the KX to flourish. Additionally, specific plans have been developed that govern end user participation in the system. This has been and will continue to be particularly important in order to vertically align enterprise goals and objectives with organizational or individual goals and objectives.

Governance is also important in light of the need to maintain secure business intelligence. Clear, constantly enforced guidelines on information requirements enable a robust KX to positively affect the AFMS.

Marketing and Communication

The AFMS KX team has produced a continuous marketing and communication plan that is a core part of a KX deployment. This includes training for those individuals who will be working directly with the new system, as well as clearly defined executive communication plans, recruitment plans, and community of practice leadership plans.

Marketing and communication of proper system uses and security requirements has been key to how Knowledge Exchange is enhancing the enterprise.

Trust Systems

A frequently overlooked aspect of knowledge-sharing is the integrity of the data. The KX Trust System validates the source of data and qualifies individuals who are contributing content. Most enterprise cultures accept that policy documents and official memos are validated if they carry the seal of the organization. However, effective Trust systems go further by assuring that all documents are current and that the source of all documents is valid.

Communities of Practice

The KX implementation model does not require a strict definition of a Community of Practice–only the more general concept that individuals are more effective when they can communicate and share with organizations and affinity groups whose interests are similar to theirs. Providing community services to a group of individuals associated with a given aspect of the organization facilitates collaboration and information-sharing. Individuals who know their particular subject well, who know other interested members, and who have a common means of communication and culture are able to respond well to the business needs of the organization.

Many "communities" have evolved in the first few months of active KX growth. These communities are sharing information, managing their dispersed teams, and conducting their daily jobs via the KX.

Performance Measures and Metrics

A well-defined program for measuring performance and defining metrics is critical to a successful KX implementation. This program must measure business effectiveness as opposed to simply creating statistical counts.

The AFMS KX team has built a great deal of measurement into the application and is beginning to customize reporting to allow executive sponsors the ability to more readily measure business impact.

Rewards and Incentives

The AFMS KX team has to date relied on more Darwinian concepts to achieve growth and enhance system usage. However in the future, a carefully considered and implemented reward and incentive plan is necessary. For example, the Navy documented the fact that knowledge-sharing amongst ships at sea rapidly increased when they were directly associated to shore-leave privileges.

Subject Matter Expertise (SME) Development

Many cultural and organizational barriers prevent knowledgeable individuals from becoming visible to the knowledge-sharing community. Due to its relative youth, the KX has yet to experience the impact of these barriers. However, the growth of expertise systems and the need to maintain content integrity should drive the identification of sanctioned "subject matter experts."

Organizational Learning

The AFMS KX team defines organizational learning as "the implementation of core interventions that transform an enterprise into a true Learning Organization." Through the principle of distributed web content management, the KX team has built flexibility into the application to allow knowledge sharing on an enterprise scale. Organizational learning deals with cultural change, knowledge sharing, and the value of intellectual capital. It overcomes resistance to change by creating ways for learners to identify and access other individuals with the know-how and experience to help them. Similarly, organizational learning provides ways for an enterprise to identify and encourage individuals who are knowledge creators and to match them with individuals who are knowledge distributors and knowledge consumers.

Enterprise Strategy

The AFMS KX team built the KX as an effective tool in vertically aligning the organization, its departments, and branches with its goals and objectives. The ability of Air Staff personnel to develop an enterprise strategy and then make those steps known to all the individuals within the organization via the KX was heretofore impossible. In addition, interventions that determine the readiness of a sub-group to accept and implement the enterprise strategy as well as determine the business case can be implemented.

Summary

The Air Force Surgeon General's Knowledge Exchange implementation is a major step in bringing the organization's knowledge or intelligence into an environment that can then allow the organization to have a true enterprise intranet, offering the ability to capture and distribute knowledge in a unique and meaningful way. This goes beyond the legacy web-based approach of posting contents and pointers to documents in a static environment and offering links to a proliferation of unconnected web sites. Instead, the implementation of the Knowledge Junction provides a mechanism for service members and providers to interact with the enterprise in a meaningful and dynamic fashion.

Knowledge Junction merges together fundamentally different forms of knowledge on the AFMS Knowledge Exchange. The Knowledge Junction approach recognizes that each user needs access to a different part of AFMS with every interaction.

When a user searches for information, the research process quickly yields not only documents in a repository but also information about who the experts are and whether there exist any collaboration threads relevant to one's interest. In addition, searches find relevant knowledge located in divergent parts of the organization, such as an item placed into the repository by a facility that is geographically and operationally removed from the user's work environment.

Going beyond the usual Web-based limitations in its creation and distribution of knowledge, Knowledge Junction takes knowledge from qualitatively different sources and makes it available to a broad range of users in a complex organization. With Knowledge Junction, the search for knowledge and the ability to share knowledge become more fluid, flexible and intuitive. The ability to organize and clarify knowledge and the ability to effectively distribute it and share it increases the power of knowledge and the capabilities, swift response time and flexibility of the organization.

CHAPTER TEN

CASE STUDY: CYBER-SECURITY INITIATIVES IN THE FEDERAL SECTOR

Introduction

Neither businesses, government agencies nor personal computer users function in a virtual fortress, impervious to the slings and arrows of the public domain. Hacking tools are freely available on the Internet–some are the same tools used by system administrators to manage their network. For example, a tool used to recover a forgotten password can be as easily used to steal a password. A tool used by to monitor a computer's activities on the Internet can be as easily used to steal the knowledge of those activities.

Whatever their intentions, hackers, crackers and script kiddies disrupt and deny services, compromise customer data, raise IT expenditures and create corporate embarrassment both internally and externally causing loss of confidence among clients, customers partners. The end result is always the same: tarnished credibility and a high cost of recovering from damage.

Loss of network connectivity, system availability and processed data have a significant impact. According to the 2002 Computer Crime and Security Survey, conducted jointly by the FBI and Computer Security Institute, respondents reported $455,848,000 in financial losses due to computer attack, principally through their Internet connection.

Once a system is attacked by viruses, worms and malicious codes, it acts as a corridor through which those codes can spread through its network and hop a ride onto the Internet superhighway. And all it takes to initiate an attack is a computer and an Internet connection.

Just as special radio channels are set up along interstate highways to enable motorists to report on any driving problems, so does the world of computer networks need an alert system to provide information on cyber-threats reported in any system, anywhere in the world. In this way, system owners, manages, and administrators can take protective action and swiftly engineer solutions to counter that threat.

Risk Assessment and Vulnerability Mitigation Through CERT and NOSC Activities

Our economy and national security depend upon an uninterrupted flow of communication providing critical information to businesses and national security decision-makers 24 hours a day. Unfortunately, our ability to keep those critical channels secure has not kept pace with our ever-increasing reliance upon the information that they provide. Over the course of the past decade, Computer Emergency Response Teams (CERT) acted to counter many of those security threats. But the CERT's ability to do so is rapidly becoming overwhelmed by the sheer mass and growing sophistication of those threats.

In the cyber-realm, security is referred to as *Information Assurance*, or IA–but today that assurance is very much in question.

Recently, a new defensive system has been initiated and applied within commercial sectors and federal agencies in an attempt to provide IA to a global network infrastructure. This new system is the Network Operations and Security Center, or NOSC. EVOLVENT associates have implemented such a center at the Department of Veterans Affairs (VA) and are currently creating the infrastructure for establishing the U.S. Army Medical Command Network Operations Security Center.

The purpose of NOSC is to go beyond the model of a reactive service triggered by particular attacks–the operating principle of CERT–and instead to provide pro-active protection at all times by combining and merging network operations personnel with IA professionals in a dynamic, mutually inclusive environment.

In addition to ensuring stable and reliable operations, a NOSC provides formal risk assessments, taking into account theft of proprietary information, sabotage of data or networks, financial fraud and computer theft. By working hand-in-hand with the network operators, the IA team develops theses assessments which detail what needs to be protected and where IA measures must be implemented. These risk assessments cannot be one-time events. Just as threats, vulnerabilities and operations are constantly transmuting, so must risk assessments be constantly updated. For instance, when an organization purchases new workstations for its employees, it is critical that the old workstations containing confidential data on their hard drives not fall into unauthorized or hostile hands. NOSC/IA professionals provide information, awareness and solutions training to prevent such occurrences.

Unfortunately, although theoretical solutions abound, there is a shortage of qualified IA personnel to oversee network infrastructures. Recently, a National Education Training Program for Infrastructure and Information Assurance was established to address this concern. However, until those new professionals are trained, there still exists a gap in the defensive postures of network and computer systems integrity. The NOSC is meant to fill this void, providing a team of IA professionals to make up for the present shortage of experienced IA personnel.

Implementing a NOSC

To address current threats, vulnerabilities, risks and IA limitations, the military services and several government agencies have already deployed NOSC solutions which have proven very effective in responding to real and potential threats. Each NOSC implements the CERT concept of incident response and threat mitigation.

Conceptually, a CERT is designed to react. It identifies a network or system attack, conducts computer forensic analysis, reports the incident to operational and legal channels as required and offers after-action recommendations to decision makers. In the main, CERT activities are not designed to monitor a total network infrastructure and user workstations on a 24/7/365 basis; that's a NOSC function.

A NOSC incorporates the CERT and provides it information by monitoring internal network activity, reviewing systems for known vulnerabilities, providing penetration testing, applying virus protection and system vulnerability fixes, offering advice and assistance, issuing threat and vulnerability warnings to network users, conducting term analysis and providing a first strike "triage" reaction capability.

With the CERT concept, NOSCs provide an IA architecture for a secure operating environment. A NOSC establishes an IA system that is under the direct control of the entity for which it is working–whether a business or a federal or military activity. Because NOSC personnel have an understanding of the organization in which they work, they are poised to provide solutions before the organization deploys a computer system or institutes configuration changes in a network.

Taking a centralized, rule-based approach, NOSC makes it easier to secure and manage networks. By aligning itself with other IA functions and CERT activities, the NOSC provides the one element that has been missing from the IA architecture: an internal IA source that understands the particular organization which it is protecting thus providing credibility to the premise that you must intimately understand what you have in order to effectively protect it.

NOSC is a cost-effective approach with a tangible and measurable return on investment (ROI). The ROI is based upon the NOSC's proactive and reactive capabilities in deterring attacks, mitigating adverse effects of such attacks and enhancing recovery operations to reduce operational downtime and associated costs. The result is decreased damage, reduced recovery costs and continued operations.

In short, NOSC is the right way to provide a centralized IA network management process that can deal with today's threats, vulnerabilities, risks and limitations ensuring continuity of operations, uninterrupted revenue streams, and protection of vital data, systems and networks.

Federal Sector Requirements

The United States Department of Defense has been concerned about the threat posed to its omnipresent and myriad computer systems by malicious outside intrusion since the early 1990s. Defense Department systems have been attacked up to 250,000 times a year. Only one out of 50 of such attacks is detected and reported. The Defense Department established its first unit to combat cyberthreats late in 1998–known as the Joint Task Force-Computer Network Defense (JTF-CND) (now known as the JTF-Computer Network Operations (JTF-CNO)–in response to a number of exercises as well as real events. Of these, there were two principal factors. One was Exercise *Eligible Receiver 97*, in which the National Security Agency (NSA) simulated an attack on Department of Defense networks, revealing numerous vulnerabilities within DOD systems, inadequate defenses and the potential for significant damage to DOD networks and systems. The other was a computer hacking attack initially attributed to suspected Iraqi agents. In addition, exercises such as the U.S. Atlantic Command's *Evident Surprise* also contributed to the increasing awareness of the vulnerability of many computer systems.

Eligible Receiver 97 was directed by the chairman of the Joint Chiefs of Staff and run from June 9 to June 13, 1997, and was the first large-scale no-warning military field exercise designed to test the ability of the United States to respond to an attack on both the United States military and civilian information infrastructures. The exercise involved simulated attacks by "opposing forces" against components of the civilian infrastructure, such as power and communications companies, as well as attacks against key defenses information systems at the Pentagon, the Joint Staff, the Department of Defense and Central Intelligence Agency, other supporting agencies and sectors of the unified combatant commands.

Eligible Receiver exploited common vulnerabilities such as bad or easily guessed passwords, operating system deficiencies, improper system configuration control, inadequate user awareness of operational security, sensitive site-related details posted on publicly accessible Internet pages and poor operator training. Although the personnel involved in launching this attack (drawn from the National Security Agency) were given no inside information, they were still able to inflict considerable simulated damage. Part of the reason for the success of this attack was because the attackers had engaged in extensive preliminary electronic reconnoitering of target agencies and sites.

Several months later, from February 1 to February 26, 1998, a number of computer attacks presumably originating from the Middle East and other locales were detected. At least 11 attacks were launched against Navy, Marine Corps and Air Force computers worldwide, primarily attempting to inflict denial of service. Later termed Solar Sunrise, these attacks exploited a well-known vulnerability in the Solaris operating system (for which a patch had been available for months). Because these attacks were launched just as the United States military forces were preparing for possible combat missions against Iraq, they elicited great concern, and an interagency investigation named Solar Sunrise was initiated. The Air Force, Army, NASA, NSA,

Department of Justice, CIA and FBI were all involved in the investigation. Despite the fact that none of the systems attacked were classified, the security breaches could have been used to disrupt Defense Department information flow during a possible Middle East war, and the investigation was one of the largest of its type ever conducted in the United States. Numerous court orders were swiftly issued, and it was discovered that the culprits were actually two California teenagers and their eighteen-year-old Israeli mentor.

Due to these incidents, the Defense Department moved quickly to take defensive measures. These measures included:

- Increasing situational awareness via a 24 hour watch center,
- Installing intrusion detection systems on key systems nodes,
- Expanding computer emergency response teams to perform alerts, critical triage and repair,
- Developing contingency plans to mitigate the degradation or loss of networks,
- Improving the Defense Department's ability to analyze data rapidly and assess attacks,
- Improving links with the FBI's National Infrastructure Protection Center and other law enforcement agencies.

On December 30, 1998, the Joint Task Force-Computer Network Defense (JTF-CND) was activated, and achieved full operational capability six months later (in June, 1999). In October, 1999, JTF-CND was assigned to United States Space Command, which was assuming the Pentagon's computer network defense mission.

The JTF-CND is located in Arlington, Virginia, alongside the Defense Information Systems Agency's Global Network Operations and Security Center. It incorporates the Defense Department's Computer Emergency Response Team (CERT) and the four service Computer Emergency Response Teams. Three of these four CERTs are stationed in the Washington, D.C., area. Originally, the JTF-CND was comprised of approximately 40 uniformed and civilian personnel, including intelligence specialists, Defense Department law enforcement personnel and counterintelligence special agents focusing on computer-related criminal activity.

Mid-2001 congressional testimony indicated that the JTF-CND is now set to grow to about 144 personnel.

A year after the JTF-CND was assigned to Space Command, Space Command gained the mission of Computer Network Attack-Offensive Information Warfare–which, on April 2, 2001, was renamed the Joint Task Force-Computer Network Operations (JTF-CNO), indicating a broader mandate.

This revised unit has embarked on building relations with other agencies, such as the National Infrastructure Protection Center (which is now proposed to become part of the Homeland Security Department) and the National Communications System, a confederation of 22 federal agencies and departments charged with ensuring the availability of a safe and viable telecommunications infrastructure. The Joint Task Force's defense computer security mission will rest to some extent on the linkages it establishes with other government agencies and private companies.

The Defense Department is confronted by on-going computer infiltration attempts that go beyond the scope of routine computer viruses and unsophisticated hacker attacks. Most publicized was an apparent incursion from Russia in 1999, seemingly originating from the Russian Academy of Sciences, which was dealt with by an investigation codenamed Moonlight Maze. This and other attacks helped spur the development of automated intrusion detection systems. These have greatly enhanced the Defense Department's ability to detect and respond to cyber-incursions.

At present, further work is at progress within the NSA to identify an intruder even before he or she enters a Defense Department system.

In 2001, there were 14,500 attacks, of which 70 made it into Defense Department computers and 3 caused damage. (These latter 3 were matched by other attacks that damaged private computer networks at the same time.) While the Defense Department seems to be making progress in its cyber-defenses, much work remains to be done in order to stay ahead of hackers, including the education of users and systems administrators alike. Many of today's problems persist because system administrators are still recalcitrant in installing routine patches either because of a lack of security training, undermanning or excessive workloads. Effective security training for system administrators would place IA on the front lines of network operations and greatly enhance any organization's security posture.

Practical Example: Department of Veterans Affairs

With 25.3 million current active veterans and a quarter of the nation's population (approximately 70 million people) eligible for VA benefits, the Department of Veterans Affairs (VA) is the second largest Cabinet Department in the United States.

Recently, the VA established a Computer Incident Response Center (VA-CIRC) in conjunction with VAST, LLC (VAST), a joint venture which includes EVOLVENT.

In a press release announcing this initiative, Dr. John A. Gauss, VA Assistant Secretary for Information and Technology said, "Complete privacy is the bedrock of this initiative, we are confident that the VAST team understands the requirements and has established the expertise, tools and technologies to satisfy all aspects of this ambitious project. Our mission is to launch a new global standard in cyber security, and we believe the right team is now in place to accomplish our ultimate 'ONE-VA' goal of protecting our customers' personal electronic information at all costs."

Along with its business partners, VAST has established and manages a state-of-the-art computer incident response center. This center is the nucleus of all VA information and Internet security operations nationwide, providing continuous protection, detection and response capabilities against threats, vulnerabilities exploitable by remote control and real-time incidents on all VA-affiliated networks. In addition, a global "early warning" information-sharing network will be implemented, in cooperation with leading elements of homeland defense, law enforcement, the federal government, vendors, universities, and laboratories providing analysis and validation of how emergencies are responded to.

John Linton, Chief Operating Officer for SecureInfo Corporation, states that "the VA's meticulous information security initiative signals a major advancement in the protection of private electronic information for the American public, and we expect that other federal agencies and global business leaders will follow this trend in the near future." He adds that "we have established a world-class computer security team that is focused on making sure that the VA, as a vital component in the lives of many Americans, is prepared to face the growing trend of computer related crime and cyber-terrorism that threatens our nation's critical infrastructures."

VA Computer Incident Response Capability team leaders stated the need for such security measures. "In today's world of Internet uncertainty, every passing week reveals another episode of malicious hackers and cyber-terrorists exploiting vulnerable networks across the globe. Through a combination of proactive prevention, real-time detection and immediate response, the VA-CIRC will now effectively protect those veterans that have protected our country throughout its history."

Practical Example:
Department of Army Medical Services & HIPAA Compliance

It is inevitable that medical networks and patient systems will be attacked. Concerned with the protection of medical information, especially with the compliance mandated by HIPAA, the Army Medical Command has taken the stance to create a centralized security management approach to security. Faced with limited resources, funding and manpower, the proposed solution to "centralized security management," is the establishment of a Network Operations and Security Center (NOSC). The NOSC concept will minimize time needed to secure systems, lower total cost of security ownership, and maximize the effectiveness of the Army Medical Command security process. While the NOSC will provide the desired security solution for the Army Medical environment, several preparatory actions had to be implemented.

- Increase DOD and Army Information Assurance (IA) compliance and awareness within each Medical Treatment Facility.
- Establish an IT repository of all Army medical systems.
- Ensure all Army medical systems were secured through the deployment of the DOD Information Technology Security Certification and Accreditation Process (DITSCAP).
- Implement, manage and enforce the DOD Information Assurance Vulnerability Management (IAVM) compliance process.
- Establish an Army Medical Command DITSCAP repository to enforce accountability of the DITSCAP requirements and to ensure over 700 medical systems are secured.
- Establish an IA operational activity to implement and manage IA processes for DITSCAP, incidents, IT registry, and so forth.

Several of the above items are successfully implemented with the IA operational activity tentatively scheduled to be located within the U.S. Army Medical Information Technology Center (USAMITC), the technology activity center for the Army Medical Command. Already possessing a premier IA program, USAMITC will be responsible for IA operational enforcement. Eventually, when the Medical Command NOSC is implemented, this process will fall under the IA Operational Activity, reporting to the Army Medical Command, and to the Army's NETCOM activity.

CHAPTER ELEVEN

CASE STUDY: UNDERSTANDING THE COST DRIVERS

In a marketplace dominated by on-going technology requirements (and their commensurate costs), executives in the public and private sectors alike are demanding return on investment from technology budgets. But how do they measure results? The language of technology executives frequently does not translate into that of the CEO or CFO; conversely, the language of finance does not translate into that of the average IT manager or CIO. Many organizations still find it difficult to make sense of their information technology infrastructure, how it is performing and what requirements they will need to plan for. With this enters the specter of costly security projects, and so it is easy to understand why managers struggle with the financial aspect of IT performance.

Yet it has never been more critical that IT play a major role in securing business intelligence. Security perspectives and requirements, twinned with the pressures of capturing and utilizing organizational knowledge, demand that IT leaders deliver business-changing performance.

Several years ago, EVOLVENT began a series of measurement studies, utilizing the Gartner Group's Total Cost of Ownership model for Distributed Computing. After having completed more than 50 studies covering four continents and over 100,000 end users, EVOLVENT's analysts have developed a proven methodology for collecting, validating and analyzing IT financial performance. The resultant recommendations for new initiatives and validation of current IT programs have helped public and private managers gain a far clearer picture of their return on investment.

As part of these measurement studies EVOLVENT analysts identify a series of best practices that, taken together, provide a recipe for improving the way the organization secures business intelligence. From standards compliance to remote monitoring and maintenance, these technology best practices provide a series of concrete steps that business managers can take to reduce costs, manage security risks, and enhance organizational knowledge sharing. By quantifying service levels and establishing a series of operational benchmarks, these studies point to effective financial strategies and risk management activities.

Gartner Group defines Total Cost of Ownership (TCO) as "a comprehensive set of methodologies, models and tools to help organizations better measure costs, manage costs, reduce costs and improve the overall value of IT investments."

When applied to IT or any other asset class/business model, a Total Cost of Ownership assessment helps managers quantify the real financial impact of that asset class. By capturing the inventory and operations cost and assessing the organizational impact of the business model, a TCO assessment can provide a complete picture for managing more efficiently and providing better service.

TCO is part of EVOLVENT's portfolio of knowledge management consulting services. EVOLVENT's past projects have demonstrated that this linkage is crucial, since TCO is a financial analysis tool that is key to aligning IT strategy with business strategy. EVOLVENT's certified experts in TCO can help define an organization's success in terms of industry best practices, end user operations costs and the cost of the fixed IT infrastructure. In other words, a TCO assessment offers managers a real view of what IT is costing the enterprise.

EVOLVENT's TCO Assessment Team also provides clients with business case analysis reports for IT outsourcing strategies and improved seat management practices. EVOLVENT's consultants work with a client's internal project teams to evaluate and document existing information technology costs and to build a strategic plan to reduce costs and improve efficiencies. EVOLVENT's unique approach provides the user with an unbiased approach, utilizing best practice tool sets for evaluation coupled with CIO-level expertise to assist in developing the client's strategic direction.

A Sample Case

In the initial phase of a recent IT re-engineering project for a large federal enterprise consisting of many distinct functions, EVOLVENT analysts conducted a Total Cost of Ownership study to establish a baseline set of performance criteria for providing IT services at various locations. Specific areas were identified, and the study recommended that the enterprise take specific corrective measures to improve performance.

Gartner identifies best practices in more than thirty specific categories. Questionnaires were utilized to gather operating practice information and to compare the quantified results to industry performance benchmarks. The TCO study pointed to several major areas where best practices implementation was at the low end of industry norms. These areas were the following:

- Operational Management Best Practices Benchmarks
- Data Management
- Performance Monitoring/Event Management
- Security
- Standards Compliance
- Customer Service Best Practices Benchmarks
- Service Desk Technology Best Practices
- Service Desk Process
- Marketing/Relationship Management

Let us look more closely at these components one at a time.

Data Management

The study revealed that data management functions were not centralized but managed at the end user level. Business intelligence or knowledge sharing was virtually non-existent, and there were many instances of disparate systems and/or locations searching for the same information. In response, the pilot re-engineering effort instituted central data analysis/information management capabilities.

Organizations that implement best practices in this area do the following:

- Centralize data management
- Use automated tools
- Minimize labor for the user

- Integrate the backup
- Deploy restoration and storage management processes

By adopting best practices in this area, the company under study would free IT staff to provide additional training and support and to gain additional skills to perform their role. In addition, best practice implementation would allow end users more time to perform their primary tasks.

The study also identified two key strategic objectives:

- Initiate centralized data management, automated tools
- Integrate the backup process, and deploy restoration and storage management processes

As a result of identifying these best practice benchmarks and the comparative performance of the organization, several key steps were taken to initiate a central data analysis process, and to add technical capabilities for backups and storage management.

Performance Monitoring and Event Management

The study revealed that this firm's problem detection technology was very limited in scope.

Organizations that implement best practices in this area do the following:

- Deploy problem detection technology
- Integrate problem detection tools with other systems management schemes
- Use redundant systems

Use of these best practices would allow IT personnel in the company under study to reduce the amount of end user time spent in chasing lost data or in downtime, and would reduce the amount of IT time required to get systems working again.

The study also identified a key strategic objective: to implement problem detection technology to enable early detection and/or prevention.

After the study identified this security and risk management deficiency, the organization moved aggressively to deploy more proactive technology and process solutions.

Security

The study revealed that information and systems security had achieved little in attaining a secure-compliant environment.

Organizations that implement best practices in this area do the following:

- Use tools and procedures that ensure proper access to data
- Use tools and procedures that prevent asset removal or tampering

Data protection and information security issues are increasingly crucial as federal information assurance guidelines become standard practice and enforcement penalties increase.

The study also identified a key strategic objective:

- To develop and implement compliant policies and procedures to ensure security and appropriate accessibility of data

Standards Compliance

The study showed that a variety of computer configurations and software versions resulted in an overly complex and costly operating environment. When IT staff have to support a variety of client configurations, the amount of time needed to troubleshoot system problems increases. In addition, most of the desktop software was manually distributed and updated. The wide variety of configurations resulted in high operating costs and high levels of peer support.

Organizations that implement best practices in this area manage diversity in client configurations, while providing flexibility for users.

The study also identified four key strategic objectives:

- To initiate centralized deployment of software and updates, patches, etc
- To implement processes to manage client system configurations centrally
- To implement an automated software distribution tool
- To develop and implement procedures and supporting processes to ensure a proper implementation and institutionalization of such a product

The development of a standard client system configuration that is locked down by the IT department, measured for reliability and performance, and reinforced by manufacturer warranties enables a much more secure infrastructure and increases users' confidence to build a knowledge-sharing environment.

Service Desk Technology and Process

The study identified the current state of service desk technologies and processes as follows:

- Only rudimentary help desk metrics were tracked
- At most sites, no formal trouble tracking or Automated Call Distribution existed
- Lack of a help desk skill inventory of personnel hindered training and resulted in a lengthened trouble resolution time

Organizations that implement best practices in this area:

- Minimize IS and end-user labor
- Ensure the quality and reliability of the problem management process

By deploying technologies that reduce the amount of staff time required to track and solve end-user problems, the firm under study could substantially reduce its operating costs. These best practices would also reduce the peer support required by many end users that is currently necessary because many end-users are taking their problems to a colleague before going to the help desk. Thus, poor help desk utilization leads to an enterprise-wide productivity drain in other functions.

By implementing processes that reduce IT staff time needs, the firm under study would model best practices in Service Desk Technologies. The result would be a reduction in operating costs and an improvement in service. And that would result in a reduction of end user dependence upon peer support.

The study also identified four key strategic objectives:

- To establish a centralized or virtual help desk function that would support a multiplicity of locations and effectively leverage resources and expertise to help a broad range of end users
- To deploy Remedy or any equivalent web-based application. This would have the result of providing access to a trouble-ticket tracking

system, which would deal with all end user problems, service requests and "how to" questions
- To utilize the application in order to monitor metrics and identify common problems
- To install a telephony system that would enable the collection of statistics such as call volume, wait time, average speed of response, call length and abandonment rate. This would greatly improve customer service
- To utilize service desk technologies in order to minimize IS and end user labor. That would ensure the quality and reliability of the process employed to solve problems

These performance improvements built a foundation for the reliability and efficiency of a knowledge exchange, and greatly empowered members of the organization to create, share and increase enterprise knowledge.

Services: Marketing and Relationship Management

The study identified the current state of services marketing and relationship management as follows:

- Service level agreements were under development
- Investment in end user training was significantly below peer and database averages, leading to high end user operations cost

This benchmark addresses the processes, techniques and methods used to improve the relationship between the IS organization and business areas, provide an IT-face to the user community and increase customer satisfaction with IT services and systems.

Implementing best practices in this area would increase customer satisfaction and improve alignment of business and technology goals and objectives. Investing in end-user training could also lead to significant benefits. Only 16% of end-users at the sites in the firm under study would, as their first step in dealing with a problem, go to the help desk. The fact that at this firm, the alignment between user goals and objectives on the one hand and IT goals and objectives on the other hand was sub-optimal was quantified through identifying peer support costs, inefficient help desk operations (reflected in high operations costs) and independent application development.

The study also identified three key strategic objectives:

- To utilize the Service Level Agreements process to facilitate communication with communications providers
- To develop processes, techniques and methods to improve the relationship between the IS organization and business areas, provide an IT-face to the user community and increase customer satisfaction with IT services and systems
- To develop and implement an effective training program for end users

Study Results

The assessment team identified seven major areas of best practice implementation that could yield in excess of $16 million in potential savings. EVOLVENT's analysts helped re-engineer the client's business model to achieve these operational efficiencies. These seven implementation areas helped reshape the development of a knowledge sharing environment where tacit and explicit knowledge diffusion was not hindered by IT operations. IT security (a major objective of the client) was also greatly enhanced by the implementation of these best practices.

In general, as companies around the world demand significant ROI from their IT departments, TCO's bench marking and "true" cost picture are a necessity for executive leaders.

A Lesson for IT to Learn

Each year, the need to accurately define the cost of IT systems grows exponentially in an ever-evolving and increasingly complex environment.

TCO is an approach that allows managers to quantify the impact of processes and expenditures. By making use of TCO assessments, managers will improve their knowledge of cost structures and service levels. The result can be a major improvement in the way that IT services are procured and delivered to the end user.

TCO and the Technology Company

Why would a technology company require a TCO study?

TCO assessments provide a great deal of important information from both a business development perspective and an efficiency perspective. An assessment provides the yardstick by which to measure what return proposed changes would bring. An assessment also identifies opportunities to improve operations to re-engineer processes in order to achieve savings, enhance performance, and measure security efforts.

An independent TCO review can provide the technology company with an unbiased third party's review. This review can identify areas where core competencies of the vendor would greatly benefit the end client. It can also identify areas where the service offering needs a partnering approach to provide the best possible service.

Summary

Why would a client organization want to launch a TCO assessment?

- To ensure that it has the complete picture of what it will cost to procure, own and use IT components
- To develop and implement a plan for IT budgeting, operations and investments
- To consolidate help functions and utilize remote technologies for service delivery and monitoring
- To consider central/enterprise procurement strategies
- To understand and document the relationship between IT investments and business value/requirements
- To validate and verify the operational impact of past and future IT expenditures
- To verify training requirements and how users can be assisted to reduce costs to the enterprise in terms of lost data and downtime

TCO studies allow an organization to gain a better view of the cost impact of how it is currently deploying information technology resources. By including user feedback and identifying operating practices, the TCO methodology allows organizations to access a rounded view of their "true" information technology costs.

The experience of enterprises has been that implementing TCO initiatives:

- Reduces costs
- Increases service levels
- Increases user satisfaction

Enterprises that successfully implement best practices in their distributed computing infrastructure *can reduce costs by as much as 56%* (Gartner, 2001). Enterprises that conduct TCO assessments have a better understanding of the cost of procuring, owning and using IT components over time. A TCO assessment also sets a baseline for creating and implementing a financial plan for IT budgeting, operations and investment planning.

PART FOUR

LESSONS LEARNED

CHAPTER TWELVE

GLOBAL ALERT NETWORK: A FIRST RESPONDER SYSTEM

Knowledge Management and National Security

The realization that knowledge management and security are essential in assuring a healthy and thriving business in any industry is not new. What is new is the transformed landscape on which we stand. After September 11, we were challenged to adopt new ways of thinking. The once-tangential realm of secure networks and information has now become a central concern.

In the aftermath of September 11, security became paramount to an unprecedented extent. Businesses lost immense amounts of data and resources, but even more than that, the culture of America changed. The open society grew a little less open. America's youthful and dynamic embrace of the world was tinged with fear.

However, new technologies can help us face security threats with renewed vigor and optimism. Here we present Global Alert Network, a proposed fully-integrated and inclusive model for first responder systems. GAN is based on the concept of knowledge management and using the particular concepts and tools of Knowledge Junction, which were described at length in Chapter Six. In doing so, GAN will gather and manage the knowledge of all elements of disaster response.

Why GAN?

Since the Department of Homeland Security was created shortly after September 11, 2001, billions of dollars have been spent to create better ways of communicating before, during and after a terrorist attack. However, despite the expenditure of so much money and the passing of so much time, a satisfactory scheme has still not yet been devised.

The Department of Homeland Security was designed to combine security, emergency response and threat detection services into one central agency. To do so, resources were pulled from the Departments of Agriculture, Treasury, Commerce, Energy, Justice, Health and Human Services, Transportation and Defense, as well as from independent agencies such as the Federal Emergency Management Agency (FEMA). The Department of Homeland Security is meant to serve as a central repository of expertise in the areas of preventing, detecting and protecting against future attacks on American soil.

Once the Department of Homeland Security coordinated all these resources, its next step was to connect these agencies with each other and with the civilian population in an on-going relationship. This would provide a medium that could provide information on preparing for, preventing and mitigating emergencies, and could alert the public when necessary. In the event of attack, the Department of Homeland Security could coordinate emergency response teams, hospitals, the military, information systems and the general public.

The Department of Homeland Security's disorganization severely limits its ability to coordinate and facilitate communication amongst local, state and federal agencies and amongst various other agencies within each level of government. Nor has the Department of Homeland Security disbursed funds effectively. This is so because the Department of Homeland Security has funneled the majority of the money to local agencies, which spend it on personnel and equipment such as biochem suits. This money would be much better spent on IT and communications projects, meant to improve cross-agency, multi-jurisdiction response to threats and emergencies. In short, the Department of Homeland Security has made little headway, and the pressure to create a successful system is only growing more urgent and acute.

The work by many of our associates have lead to the proposed system to directly and clearly implement IT initiatives that are necessary to attaining true homeland security. Global Alert Network (GAN) is an all-inclusive communication system that would link all-important aspects of public security, and would be a key method keeping everyone, including the general public, informed of threats or impending attacks.

Global Alert Network: A Strategic Plan

Although various efforts have been made to upgrade America's anti-terror capabilities, they still have a significant Achilles' heel: the fact that these efforts are not sufficiently coordinated and inter-communicative.

Many government agencies, such as law enforcement, intelligence, diplomatic, military, news services and public health agencies are involved in protecting the population from terrorism and in responding to contingencies or disasters. In combination with the Department of Homeland Defense, they serve as the essential organizations protecting the general public.

Unfortunately, what is still missing is an information technology infrastructure that integrates all agencies involved in providing information about emergency and disaster preparedness so that together they can provide optimal up-to-date information and engage in coordinated planning. A system that can disperse critical information in order to help everyone respond adequately in the event of a disaster has yet to be developed. Yet such a multi-sector, integrated system serving as a national framework for federal, state and local governments, private industry and the public are crucial to maintaining preparedness against acts of terror and other disasters.

It is true that the Department of Homeland Security has introduced a coding system whose purpose is to standardize the information streaming in from various agencies. That integration relies on risk assessments, which are key to determining what security strategies to employ. Because qualitative assessments are more accurate than quantitative calculations, qualitative assessments are necessary to this integration process. And the integration of information, technology, people and processes must include modules of prevention and preparedness, detection, early and sustained response and recovery.

The Department of Homeland Security's coding system is a welcome and important beginning to the creation of an all-inclusive alert network. However, it lacks two key components:

- The people and processes parts of responding to a contingency or disaster.
- The technological infrastructure that is meant to integrate vital and time-sensitive information is ineffective.

GAN could provide these vital services. GAN could effectively create an integrated data infrastructure by connecting government agencies, law enforcement, transportation authorities, weather experts, healthcare workers and the general public.

Background

GAN would provide a comprehensive and effective means of integrating information, technology, people and processes to deal with potential disasters. GAN would create a common open architecture, vocabulary, context and structure about threats and actions. It would provide various agencies with various levels of access and provides the public with comprehensive information. This information would be presented on a GAN television channel.

In its *White Paper 5*, the Department of Justice speaks to the need for critical infrastructure coordination:

> "[The military and the economy] are also increasingly reliant upon certain critical infrastructure and upon cyber-based information systems. Critical infrastructures are those physical and cyber-based systems essential to the minimum operations of the economy and government. They include, but are not limited to, telecommunications, energy, banking and finance, transportation, water systems and emergency services, both government and private.
>
> Many of the nation's critical infrastructures have historically been physically and logically separate systems that had little interdependence. As a result of advances in information technology and the necessity of improved efficiency, however, these infrastructures have become increasingly automated and interlinked. These same advances have created new vulnerabilities to equipment failures, human error, weather and other natural causes, and physical and cyber attacks.
>
> Addressing these vulnerabilities will necessarily require flexible, evolutionary approaches that span both the public and private sectors, and protect both domestic and international security. Because of our military strength, future enemies, whether nations, groups or individuals, may seek to harm us in non-traditional ways including attacks within the United States.
>
> Our economy is increasingly reliant upon interdependent and cyber-supported infrastructures and non-traditional attacks on our

infrastructure and information systems may be capable of significantly harming both our military power and our economy. It has long been the policy of the United States to assure the continuity and viability of critical infrastructures. President Bush intends that the United States will take all necessary measures to swiftly eliminate any significant vulnerability to both physical and cyber attacks on our critical infrastructures, including especially our cyber systems."

Threats are ever-present. But not every threat is legitimate. GAN would focus on understanding threats following the guidelines established by the Department of Homeland Security. GAN would answer the following questions about any threat:

- To what degree is the threat information *credible*?
- To what degree is the threat information *corroborated*?
- To what degree is the threat *specific and/or imminent*?
- How grave are the *potential consequences* of the threat?

Integrating data from different constituencies such as government agencies, response organizations, healthcare facilities and the general public during a major event is critical to the answering these questions. Unfortunately, the Department of Homeland Security has not yet achieved this goal. Press coverage of the recent anthrax attacks showed how sorely lacking was the integration of basic surveillance, communication and research.

On the other hand, successful use of a GAN-type construct can be seen in the response of the Centers for Disease Control to the threat of bio-terrorism. In partnership with representatives of local and state health departments, federal agencies, and medical and public health professional associations, the CDC has developed a strategic plan to deal with the deliberate dissemination of destructive biological or chemical agents. This plan continuously made recommendations on how to reduce the United States' vulnerability to biological and chemical terrorism through preparedness planning, detection, surveillance, laboratory analysis, emergency response and communication systems. Training and research are integral components for achieving these aims. And the success of the plan also hinges upon strengthening the relationships between medical and public health professionals and on building new partnerships amongst emergency management, the military and law enforcement professionals. This model of integration and coordination is the bedrock of the GAN concept.

GAN Connections

Considering how many people, processes, places and systems are involved in security, the goal of inter-operability is not too easy to attain. When the World Trade Center Towers fell on September 11, the large antenna atop Tower 2 came down, cutting off communication amongst rescue workers, government officials, transportation authorities, hospitals and mobile communications for the general public. During the sniper attacks in the Washington, DC area in 2002, police officials in Maryland, Virginia and Washington, DC, had difficulty communicating because their radios were on different bandwidths. And most recently, during the power outage in the northeastern United States and Canada, communication was next to impossible.

In addition to the major threat that communication loss poses to security, the uncertainty and fear that it engenders can also be very dangerous and destabilizing. By providing a comprehensive and secure site from which to acquire information, warnings, and evacuation plans and instructions, GAN could help public fear subside.

GAN on the National and Global Level

GAN could integrate information and then disseminate it amongst local, state, federal and international agencies. It could also function in an advisory capacity to the general public (as required by federal mandates). In doing so, GAN would work closely with the Department of Defense as well as with local, state and federal agencies, amongst them public health departments, FEMA (within the Department of Homeland Security) and the CDC.

GAN could also support various operations on a global level, utilizing a GAN channel on television and on the Internet. National agencies, including the Department of Defense, could utilize GAN's capabilities, tailoring them in order to deploy them for a wide variety of purposes.

As a state-of-the-art information and communication infrastructure, GAN would be central to the success of any major response to terrorist or other such incidents.

Technology Infrastructure

GAN's architecture captures and integrates critical information, which it then aggregates for the purpose of analysis. GAN can uncover abnormal occurrences of events within specific at-risk populations. Should such occurrences warrant an alert and are consistent with a BW/CW event, then the data flow could change while GAN notified command and control authorities.

Altered data flows provide data to experts distant from the scene in order to elicit their evaluation in regard to what steps to take in order to mitigate or even avoid risk. GAN would make it possible to combine medical data with data from other domains in order to establish a comprehensive picture of the area in question. This combined data would then be placed on the GAN infrastructure, giving command and control authorities a clear picture of the event and allowing for distribution of information to the public.

Government

GAN could integrate local, state and federal government emergency and disaster systems into one powerful system. Public and private agencies of all disciplines participating in the GAN would be able to share information and ideas.

Government and commercial agencies could work together to define the knowledge management processes necessary to giving decision-makers a full view of vital information. GAN could integrate federal, state and local emergency preparedness information and systems, including the Homeland Security Advisory System, which provides homeland security general information, threat conditions and response measures. (See the March 11, 2002 Homeland Security Presidential Directive 3 white paper published by the Office of the Press Secretary.)

Health

Should a biological attack be suspected, GAN could then support first responders as they execute their functions. GAN could record patients' symptoms, transfer data to analysis centers, perform real-time epidemiological studies, and invoke command and control system and emergency response systems. Operationally, the Global Alert Network would use and integrate information from different data domains and networks that usually do not share information, in order to deal as effectively as possibly with any attack.

Utilizing new, state-of-the-art security VPN and encryption technologies, GAN would be able to use an information portal to equip the military command and control system with integrated secure, information services and also provide information to the general public.

For example, GAN would be able to make it possible for professionals to record or review clinical information. In addition, with the help of allied software, GAN would provide critical battle management and command and control data to higher echelons of control through a "reachback capability" designed to support sustained quality medical support for national surveillance .

GAN would provide documentation about health threats and/or biological and chemical events that place military forces or the general population at risk. In addition, GAN would be able to provide comprehensive information on health risks, including environmental risks, facing Americans, such as forces deployed by the Department of Defense.

GAN's reachback capability would provide key medical, occupational and environmental information to medical authorities. In this way, GAN would integrate patient evaluation, epidemiological analysis and medical command and control amongst a broad range of agencies such as coalition forces, government agencies and civilian medical treatment facilities.

GAN is designed to be able to record and review clinical information about individual patients that might indicate potential chemical or biological attack. That information could then be shared or "rolled up" for automated analysis.

This analysis would need to occur quickly, in order to allow early identification and mitigation of any problem. GAN would improve the documentation of the healthcare delivered and the ability of agencies to respond to threats. These functions would bear some positive side-effects, such as better continuity of patient care and the reduction of illness and death in the event of attack or endemic event by means of risk avoidance.

A subchannel of GAN TV devoted to health, www.healthalertnetwork.com, would serve as a portal for health information and alerts in several ways. As clinical data was gathered and aggregated from across targeted regions, real-time analysis could be performed on a rolling, 24-hour basis.

Symptom arrays would be mapped to a backdrop of symptom patterns of possible bio-warfare agents. An alert would be generated when the spatial or temporal pattern of the data indicated suspected activity. The alert would be sent through the secure GAN, which would then help disseminate the details that caused the alert and would call upon various experts to review the information that led to the alert.

These experts, who might be located nationally or internationally, would collaborate and initiate courses of actions to either confirm or refute the possibility of an attack or other incident. If such an attack or incident were confirmed, GAN's notification system could then alert local, state and national authorities and then allow for real-time, secure collaboration.

Adjunct analysis from experts might then modify the course of action. This information would be shared with command and control authorities along with other information, in order to give them a consolidated operational picture from which they can make decisions as to the appropriate tactical response in order to avoid or mitigate risk.

Other Aspects of GAN

1. General Public

GAN would serve as an advisory portal for officials to release information to the general public as well as specific information for a particular populace struck by natural disaster or terrorist incident. Through its messaging services, GAN itself could send alerts to people located in the affected area. Evacuation policies, bio-hazard precautions, reporting center requirements, and so forth, would be established by command and control authorities and then posted to GAN, which would distribute the information, interacting with and utilizing existing local, state and federal alert systems in the area.

GAN.TV could become a primary site for reporting on calamities, dispensing a wide variety of emergency response information. It could assist authorities and decision-makers to manage public reaction to threats and disasters by providing emergency preparedness information and training as well as general response information in the event of a threat or an actual emergency.

2. Nuclear/Biological/Chemical

GAN would maintain information about the technological and medical capabilities required to counter nuclear, biological and chemical threats.

GAN would be able to integrate the medical management of chemical, biological and radiological/nuclear casualties in order to enhance survival and expedite a return to normal operations.

GAN could provide officials with information on biological defense vaccines that supply inventory (vaccines, antibodies, drugs, diagnostic technologies) and provide training materials for management of chemical, biological and radiological casualties.

Information on pre- and post-exposure countermeasures could be disseminated via GAN.

3. Environment and Transportation

GAN could be integrated with current weather alert systems. Geographic information related to incidents or disasters would be shown on GAN. Monitoring data for biological agents would be coordinated through GAN.

GAN would provide transportation updates and collect transportation-related information, as well as monitor, redirect or constrain transportation systems.

4. Agricultures

United States Food and Drug Administration (FDA) notices could be posted on GAN. Recalls of food, medicine or other products could be posted on the GAN.

5. Conclusion

In September 2003, the Department of Homeland Security committed millions of dollars to emergency operations centers. These allocated funds for development and research through the Federal Emergency Management Agency were meant to improve emergency preparedness and management. The goal was to provide support and telecommunications capabilities that promote flexibility, sustainability, security, survivability and interoperability.

In doing so, the Department of Homeland Security is taking action to secure the well being of the federal government and the general population. It is ensuring protection, communication and security throughout a nationwide system. It also provides for business continuity and recovery methods.

GAN fits this model, combining the factors involved with knowledge management and interconnectivity, using technology to help people and their knowledge get together.

Government, financial institutions, military, healthcare organizations and commercial sectors are taking steps to secure their organizations.

Technology cannot fix all of the problems involved in emergency response. Fear cannot be controlled and its consequences cannot be predicted. However, with a more reliable network to depend on, we can take steps toward controlling the fear and responding to unprecedented threats in this brave new world.

Repeatedly, scientists and mathematicians have made arcane discoveries that afterwards have become exceedingly real. The most famous of these is the formula $e=mc^2$, which referenced a strange world where, in tandem, time slows down and speeds up, and space contracts and expands. Less than fifty years after this theory was set down, it turned into spectacular and terrible reality with the implementation of the atom bomb. This demonstrates the power of that most intangible of assets, knowledge.

In the GAN model, we can see this power of applied knowledge and of knowledge management. Our greatest resources, weapons and defenses are all, basically, knowledge. Knowledge turns raw materials into weaponry and strategies. Knowledge creates power out of movement, innovation out of chaos and implementation out of information. When we see a smart bomb home in on its target, when we utilize a computer that engages in hundreds of millions of independent actions per second, we are watching the reification of knowledge.

Basically, we live in a matrix of knowledge. All reality is the communication of knowledge–whether that knowledge is a stone (not exceedingly useful) or a computer processor (significantly useful).

In order to carry out the terror attack of 9/11, the perpetrators needed knowledge. Without knowledge, everything else they had would have been trivial. When America and its allied forces conquered the armies of Iraq, they did so with men and material–but none of that would have succeeded without knowledge.

Knowledge builds cities and empires. Knowledge can destroy them and knowledge can defend them. The proposed GAN system is a vast knowledge management system that coordinates all aspects of defense and rescue work, gathering and providing knowledge. Today, more than ever, war is based on knowledge. To knock out the enemy, knock out his knowledge infrastructure. A vast army without the knowledge imparted by commanders is useless–this was the outcome of America destroying the electronic communication between Iraqi military leaders and their troops. On the other hand, a relatively small force of people who have knowledge and a connection to leaders can impose significant casualties, as is the case now when relatively few and poorly armed combatants are killing Americans in conquered Iraq. They make maximum use of their limited facilities through knowledge, whether it be surveillance or penetration of Allied intelligence.

That is why a system like the proposed GAN is so important and can be so powerful. It is a system that gathers and provides knowledge. Without knowledge, the body politic is like a body that is not receiving coordinated information from the brain. It may be magnificently built, but it is feeble and useless. With knowledge, even a relatively weak body can carry out significant, directed and effective strategies.

When we look at resources in terms of knowledge, many significant insights emerge. Those insights themselves are knowledge that we can leverage to become that much more effective and powerful. This is the strength of GAN: it recognizes and utilizes the fact that the organized and purposeful sharing of knowledge is crucial to America's struggle against the forces of destruction. As important as material and financial resources, knowledge is the backbone of intelligent, composed and directed action, as well as of positive morale and commitment. Providing the proper management and distribution of knowledge, the proposed GAN system makes us stronger, more capable and more committed.

AFTERWORD

It was a moment that trembled upon the cusp of time. When the two airliners plunged into the sides of the World Trade Center Towers, we watched the images on the television screen with a dull horror. And when the towers came plunging down in a nest of their own spectral smoke, we could not believe what we were seeing. The great building sheared down, smoothly and cleanly. Nothing was large enough to speak to the enormity and tragic majesty of those silently collapsing towers.

It was the equinox of America facing the winter of a diminished greatness, confidence and faith in herself. For the first time, acts of terror were not events that happened to foreigners overseas, but acts that reached into our cities, hearts, fears and dreams. The America that rose from her knees on September 12 was irrevocably different, sadder and wearier than the America that had brashly and blithely assumed its own strength invulnerability. For a few teetering days, all of America felt that it had no security. Even as Americans stepped back from the brink of the existential precipice, from staring into the face of mortality and woe, they knew that nothing could return to what it had been before.

In the months that followed, security became the shibboleth of America. President Bush announced a Homeland Security Department. John Ashcroft declared new policies granting the government new powers to collect information and conduct surveillance.

But what is security? In the rush to recover, react and hold back this invasion across the borders of our lives, much was done that addressed the wrong problem, or addressed it wrongly. There was action but not enough direction. There was intention but not enough information. There was the willingness to spend money but not the knowledge of what to spend it on. There was the drive to donate time and effort, but no clarity on how. There was a resolution to face the enemy, but a question of who the enemy is.

It is not surprising that the drive to secure our nation, businesses, citizens and infrastructure has seemed confused–because it is confused. Those with the loudest and most demagogic voices, calling for cosmetic and symbolic change, have the ear of the American public, because all others seem unsure.

What is security? What are strategies for security? What are the threats and how do we meet them? How much do we rely on technology and how much on changes in procedure and awareness? What is our goal and what is the road to take us there?

This book has addressed these questions and, we believe, supplied clear, functional, and often simple-to-implement ideas. Security is process, not installation of technology. Security involves commitment, understanding and vigilance. Most of all, we have argued, security means that we look at knowledge in new ways, realizing that the most critical capital of business and government is knowledge.

In this information age, knowledge is power. Knowledge can build, and it can destroy as surely as a gun ever could. Knowledge is as valuable as money ever could be. Knowledge is what gives a business its proprietary edge, and what gives the government its ability to battle our adversaries.

The process of security is the proper management of knowledge. An enterprise that uses knowledge effectively creates an environment in which to share that information, and in which access to that information is proprietary.

Like knowledge management, good security practices are human-based. In Bruce Schneier's words, "If you think technology can solve your security problems, then you don't understand the problems and you don't understand the technology." Among other things, it is people who must understand information, interpret it and respond to it.

Security systems rely on the human element. Without training, that element is often inadequate. A survey of 1200 British office workers revealed that when creating a password, almost half chose their own name or that of a pet or family member, and others created passwords based on the names Darth Vader and Homer Simpson. Nothing can guarantee total security, if for no other reason that nothing can guarantee the eradication of human frailty.

Relying primarily on the technological fix can degrade our security. If we rely on wizardry, we will grow insensitive to the ways that it can be circumvented. For instance, if we create a system of identification by use of a identification card with our photograph, a card can be stolen, and in response, the victim needs to get a new card. But if we create a powerful biometric system of identification, in which an ID card identifies us by our fingerprints and the card bearing someone's fingerprint is stolen, what is he to do? Purchase a new set of fingerprints? Not very likely. A poor security system is "brittle," in the words of Bruce Schneier. It fails easily (like the stolen biometric ID card), and when it does, it can cause a great deal of havoc. On the other hand, a good security system "fails well"–it fails slowly so that one can recover, and it fails with the least amount of damage.

When we focus on technology so intensely that we fail to see the context of reality surrounding that technology, we are setting ourselves up for failure. A "bad guy" does not need to counter our sophisticated technology, and he would be a fool to fight fair–the "bad guys" are not fools.

When we secure our businesses and manage its knowledge we employ technology as our tool and servant. Whether our business is the defense of the country or leasing cars, our business must be secure against negative forces, and open to those whose participation contributes to the enterprise and everyone associated with it.

The theme of this book has been securing business intelligence. It is our hope that you have gained information from this book, attained insight and have been inspired to take positive and conclusive action to secure your business intelligence. In closing, we wish you the very best of luck and success in your endeavors–and may your success ultimately benefit all good men and women.

APPENDIX A

IN THE MIND OF THE CYBER-CRIMINAL

"On the Internet, everyone is an equal until they prove themselves to be a moron."—Emmanuel Goldstein

There are many flavors of cyber-criminals, and within each flavor there are specialties and sub-specialties.

Here we will speak of that broad category of cyber-criminals called "hackers"–a category that some (generally hackers) deny has any criminal implications at all. A long and innocent time ago, hackers were merely inventive and creative computer programmers who could work their way in and out of programs that would baffle other, more ordinary men. But with the passage of time, these exploits were directed increasingly against unknowing targets. Whereas some hackers merely wanted the thrill of the hunt, of the accomplishment and of the ego boost, others may want your money, to crash your system or to use your system as a launching pad from which they will launch destructive attacks.

Hackers–the ones who are not out-and-out criminals–see themselves as visionaries and as fighters in the vanguard for freedom and an open society. They are technologically sophisticated (compared to the rest of us), and the virtual world of cyberspace is their playground. At the same time they treat it as an enemy. They use the technology to proclaim their protest against the secrecy that, they say, they so deplore.

There is nothing brilliant or worth boasting about in shoplifting from Hecht's. It can also be nerve-wracking, since there are guards and various buttons that can set off an alarm. But what if you could sneak into Hecht's in the middle of the night? What if you could go where you weren't allowed to go, straight into the accounting department or into the president's office? What if you could riffle through the filing cabinets, peer into the desk drawers, glance at the bankbook? If you felt particularly mischievous, maybe you would leave a clue that you were there. When the secretary turned on her computer the next morning, the screen saver would read "Larry was here." You could teach others how you did it. You could share the secrets of the door lock, circumventing the store alarm.

You might start to see yourself as a maverick, an iconoclast. Now your break-ins are no longer a mere personal thrill. You are challenging society–no, you are helping society. "Look," you say, "I was here, so tighten up your security. I'm a teenage Robin Hood, but the next guy who comes here might be a bad guy who wants to harm you."

Let a veteran and state-of-the art hacker speak for himself. He is Eric Corley, editor-in-chief of *2600: The Hacker Quarterly*, who also hosts a weekly New York radio program entitled "Off the Hook." He describes himself as a person who breaks into other people's systems but causes no damage. Mr. Corley calls himself Emmanuel Goldstein because, he explains, "I believe everyone should be given the opportunity to name themselves. That name should reflect something about who you are and what you believe in and stand for. Emmanuel Goldstein is that for me, and for those who want to learn why, get a copy of George Orwell's *1984* and see for yourself." In George Orwell's dystopian classic about a totalitarian state that rules in the name of "Big Brother," Emmanuel Goldstein is the enemy that the state creates and against which it directs the populace's hatred.

There have always been those on the fringes of society who see themselves as idealists whom society has rejected. Emmanuel Goldstein is the latest incarnation of this romantic figure. The line between non-conformity and law-breaking is not always clear.

In a society that celebrates aberrant behavior, Mr. Goldstein has to make a stretch in order to portray himself as the targeted victim of society. And since the activity that he engages in is not philosophizing or challenging the political establishment but breaking into other people's computers, one detects a hubris, an adolescent narcissism, an inflated self-importance and sense of wounded righteousness.

"Hackers, in their idealistic naiveté, reveal the facts that they discover, without regard for money, corporate secrets or government coverups," states Mr. Goldstein. And the purpose of hacking is "to seek knowledge, discover something new." This translates into being "the first one to find a particular weakness in a computer system or the first to be able to get a certain result from a program." Goldman says mournfully, "It's a sad commentary on the state of our society when someone who is basically seeking knowledge and the truth is assumed to be up to something nefarious."

Goldstein rhapsodizes about his own adventures, "My main interest has always been phones and rarely does a day pass when I don't experiment in some way with a phone system, voice mail system, pay phone or my own telephone. I've always been fascinated by the fact that we're only a few buttons away from virtually anyone on the planet and I hope that I never lose that sense of marvel. One of the most amazing things I ever got involved in was routing phone calls within the network itself—known as blue-boxing. You can't do that as easily any more, but it was a real fun way to learn how everything was connected—operators, services, countries, you name it. And in the not-too-distant past, there were so many different sounds phones made depending on where you were calling. Now they tend to be standardized rings, busies, etc. But the magic hasn't disappeared, it's just moved on to new things…satellite technology, new phone networks and voice recognition technologies…. While I've spent a great deal of time playing with phones, I get the same sense of fun from computer systems and have invested lots of time exploring the Internet."

And Goldstein concludes with the rousing clarion call, "As long as the human spirit is alive, there will always be hackers. We may have a hell of a fight on our hands if we continue to be imprisoned and victimized for exploring, but that will do anything but stop us."

Mr. Goldstein's attitude is a sense of superiority encapsulated in his observation that "on the Internet, everyone is an equal until they prove themselves to be a moron." Rather than being an apostle of the human spirit, Mr. Goldstein has chosen to judge the world according to his own idiosyncratic standards, and found it wanting.

Just as the line from non-conformist to narcissistic Robin Hood is unclear, so is the border between a man such as Emmanuel Goldstein and hackers who are interested in more overtly criminal trespass.

One of the many websites run by and for hackers is a site called ccpower.com. A long message on the home page informs the reader that "our purpose is not to offend but to educate and inform," and goes on to state that "anything contained on this site deal with [sic] activities and devices which would be in violation of various federal, states and local laws if actually carried out or constructed. The webmasters of this site do not advocate the breaking of any law..."

When you click to get on the site proper, there is an introductory clip, which consists of a green globe floating across the screen from left to right, as dark music plays ominous chords and the following message appears on the screen, phrase by phrase: "They lied about us...arrested us ...and outlawed us...but cannot keep us out!... They cannot shut us down! ... We are the power of the underground."

Are these Chinese students working in the human rights movement? Are they perhaps undercover agents in Somalia buying slave children and setting them free or an organization that has infiltrated terrorist groups in Gaza City and Damascus? Let's get on the site and find out.

"Click here," we are invited, to get "a collection of some scanned (sample) credit cards for information purposes ONLY." Other resources are "Here is some Trojan ports," "Bank list Credit Card bank issuer list," "Huge word lists, you can use it for brute force" (a method used to discover passwords).

CCPower also directs one to other sites that provide hacker's software tools and other important hackers' aids. At present, there are about 2500 pieces of hacker code that are widely available on the Internet.

And some helpful Internet courses have been posted. One is "Hacking for Newbies." The topics under discussion are DOS commands, ii. Staying Anonymous, iii. Ports, iv. Bios hacking, and v. remote administration programs (trojans)." The section on trojans states, "Trojans are programs which open up a backdoor so a client and [sic] access it. On the Internet today there are lots programs but I recommend getting either Sub Seven (easy to use and a lot of features) or Back Orifice (not so easy to use but a lot of features). Make sure you disable you antivirus when dealing with these programs because it detects them as virus' but they are not as long as you don't double click on the server. What these programs do is when you give a person server.exe on disk and he clicks on it, then it opens up a backdoor which you can connect to. Once the person has double clicked on server.exe you open up the client and type in his IP address and it connects to it. *Then you can do a lot of things.* [emphasis added] I cant explain all the features of the program just read the help file or download a tutorial on the program from the net, there are many. just goto www.google.com and search for Sub seven or Back Orifice.

"These programs also contain a exe called editserver. this program allows you to edit the way the server or trojan looks and what is does. for example: I can change the icon to a bitmap and when the victim clicks on it I can make it on a picture and at the same time install the trojan.

"Trojans are a very good way of getting remote access to a system, and I recommend that you read a lot about them before you use them. Its very simple to learn about Trojans, I recommend you download Sub Seven or Netbus if its your first time or Back Orifice is you want more control."

Another tutorial, "Exploiting 101–The Basics," disingenuously states, "On your exploiting journey, you may also come across confidential information from members, such as home addresses, credit card info etc. I know I have, many times over. I even found a hole where I could have the checks of site referrals sent to my account! Never use this information to your personal gain! This will be considered theft and misuse of personal information, and can get you into serious trouble…"

Incidentally, the instructor confirms the fact that the flood of information available on the Internet presents hackers with a cornucopia of opportunity. He enthuses, "I love google. I embrace googling. You should too. Make googling your hobby! Type in a path or exploit, and see what you get, you will be surprised! It will lead you to access logs, vulnerability reports, cool sites, etc. Whatever you find and think is useful, copy to your exploit list…"

While this site's goals and deeds are criminal, it serves as a friendly "virtual reality" community. Those who wish to volunteer their services as aop's (?)–which is to say, helping users break into sites, steal credit card numbers, and the like–are advised that their goal must be to provide "a pleasant place for users and a good line trading as well as generating the best skill team ever," and are exhorted, "you need to be a patient, honest [sic!], legit person as well as a kind person … we hate rude people."

One of these forums is called "Newbie Questions," and the site introduces it with this text: "This is the newbie palace, [sic] It's all about getting started, we were just like you when we first started. If you want to post absolutely any question, even if it's the world stupidest question, don't worry no one will even laugh at it, in fact all of us will try our best to help you."

Here are some excerpts from online chats:

"Pedro: Hi all, I work in the LaTourista hotel here inPeru and I have access to all ccs [credit card information] with full info, i'm looking for paypal, anyone interested ??? msg me !!! I verify first!"

"traderx: I work at a credit card collection agancy and we get there banking information I need someone to drop money in and send me half we split 50/50 pls don't ripping…loosers, I know when someone's a ripper so don't waste my…time"

"newbie: what I have to type to get cc [credit card] info?

helper: type !cc

newbie: !cc

Ccs': newbie!cc Name: Yukio XXXXXXXX |Address: X-X-X-XXX |City: Koduru-shi |State: Tokyo |Zip: XXX-XXXX \Phone: N/A \Country: Japan |CardType: American Express |Card Number:XXXXXXXXXXXX XXXX" (In other words, with some avuncular help, the "newbie" succeeded in stealing credit card information.)

"newbie: wont I get caught if I use these???

helper: mabe

helper: mabey

helper: if your smart you wont get caught

newbie: how can I not get caught baby

helper I boaught at least 20,000$ worth of stuff

helper: I donno figure it out:P

newbie: aww :-("

newbie 1: what is this site about

newbie 2: why does all this look like BS to me?

Helper: !chk XXXXXXXXXXXXXXXX XXXX [checking a credit card for validity]

CcVeR: Helper [X XXXXXXXXXXXXXXXX XXXXXX] This transaction has been Declined.

newbie 1: I dunno

newbie 1: looks the same to me

newbie 1: or illegal

Helper: it is ILLEGAL

Helper: so what if its illegal?

newbie 1: then what do I do iwht it

newbie 1: I like illegal

Helper: lol [lots of laughs]

Helper: search a valid cc

Helper: and use it

Helper: lol

Helper: :|

newbie 1: no way

newbie 2: how the hell do you confirm these cc's?

newbie 2: especially the cvv2? [card number expiry date]

newbie 1: anyone know where I can get up to date direct tv files

newbie 2: these bots [automatic response generators that facilitate access to credit card information] have merchant accounts or what?

newbie 1: I cant find...except pay sites

newbie 1: anyone know of a channel or server that has a lot of good direct tv hu card files and info

Hackers have a few powerful advantages on their side. The first is that once they are provided with some software that does their hacking for them, they don't have to know what they're doing. Another advantage is the sheer size of the Internet.

Imagine that the year is 1950 and some felonious individual has conceived the following strategy. He will choose a couple of keys and go from house to house, jiggling the keys to unlock the front door. Assuming that he can, he will break into the house and, in order to keep the householder from suspecting a robbery, he will take only a dime per household. Let's say that his keys can open up one out of every hundred doors. Let's say that he manages to try five hundred doors per night, which takes him a substantial amount of time. So every night he breaks into five houses and earns fifty cents.

Let's take the same individual and introduce him to the digital world of 2004. This time he will use an automatic electronic key to break into private computers. Let's say that the key opens up one out of every thousand computers. But it can try to breach the security of a million computers in just an hour. That evening, the burglar allows his key to roam through the world of the Internet for eight hours. By morning, as the burglar was sleeping, the key tested eight million computers connected to the Internet and now alerts the burglar that it is able to break into eight thousand computers. Now he sets another automated program into effect and is able to steal information that is equivalent to the worth of a dime per computer. That comes out to $800.

Another advantage that the hacker has is that he is not in a rush. He can plan his entire campaign at his leisure, then set his computer program to automatically scan the Internet for him.

And yet another advantage he has is that he is virtually invisible. Even if he is caught pilfering the computer of some victim, the likelihood of something happening to him is small.

These hackers do more than steal a dime from your computer. There is much that they can do, including installing a secret backdoor that will give them access to your computer any time they want it, the ability to control your computer, access your files and read your every keystroke, and the ability to take over your computer in tandem with thousands of others in order to launch a "denial of service" attack.

There are anti-hacker sites that contain a great deal of information that is extremely useful to those who are fighting hacking–and, unfortunately, also provides very useful information to hackers. Hideaway.net, for instance, presents these descriptions of articles one can read on its web site:

> Prolific hacker group Gobbles have posted some disturbing claims on the Bugtraq security mailing list–namely, that they were recruited by the RIAA to develop a virus/worm hybrid for combating music piracy....
>
> Outlook users should be wary of Sobig, a new email worm that has begun spreading rapidly in the past twenty-four hours....
>
> Security firm AtStake has released an advisory for an obscure flaw in the implementation of Ethernet device drivers tat could lead to information leakage....
>
> A security blunder at PR firm Carmichael Lynch left customer databases and other sensitive files exposed for over six months, according to Wired....
>
> Hard drives containing the Social Security numbers of some 500,000 members of the military and their families, along with addresses, credit card numbers, and other personal data, were stolen from TriWest healthcare Alliance offices last week....
>
> A vigilante hacker in the US has taken control of two web domains, jehad.net and jehadonline.org, which pointed to sites used by Al-Qaeda to claim responsibility for terrorist attacks....
>
> Microsoft has issued a critical security update for a flaw in the Windows shell that affects all versions of XP....

Honeynet is an organization that sets up websites that look vulnerable and thus attractive to hackers. These websites are called "honeypots," and when a hacker attacks such a honeypot, honeynet personnel can track every move he makes. Their purpose is not to track down individual hackers (it would make no more sense to do that than to track down every ant at an outdoor picnic), but to study the hackers' latest methodologies: "It is our goal to learn the tools, tactics and motives of the blackhat community and share these lessons learned. It is hoped that our research will benefit both list members and the security community." They have three goals: to raise awareness, to distribute information helping others to better secure and defend their resources and to provide the technology and methods of information gathering.

Honeynet's comment on its first goal, raising awareness, is telling: "To raise awareness of the threats and vulnerabilities that exist in the Internet today. We raise awareness by demonstrating real systems that were compromised in the wild by the blackhat community. *Many people believe it can't happen to them. We hope to change their minds"* [emphasis added]. As professionals in the field state repeatedly, the question is not whether your site or your system will be violated–the only question is when–and the likelihood is that, whether or not you are aware of it, your system has most likely been probed numerous times and probably has been penetrated already.

Over ninety percent of businesses with computer systems have reported attempts (successful or thwarted) to breach those systems.

The only way hoodlums in Harlem can pose a threat to you is if you walk into Harlem. Today hoodlums can be living in Harlem, New York, or Haarlem, Holland, London, England, or London, Connecticut. Wherever you are, you are in their neighborhood.

Hackers are here to stay: the script kiddies, the crackers (professional criminals), the elite coders and virus writers. Even the most benign have no compunctions about violating your system, and the least benign of them have no compunctions about compromising and damaging your system. It is not a question of whether or not you want to get involved. We are all in a hostile environment–as much as a person who walks through Harlem at two in the morning, whether or not he wants to be. However, if he happens to be carrying a Colt .45 and is accompanied by an armed guard while a satellite monitors his exact location and at the slightest sign of trouble a distress signal flashes to a group of police officers trained to react immediately, then he stands a very good chance of walking through those mean streets without incurring any danger. You don't have to do anything as dramatic. But inaugurating an integrated security system can easily be as effective.

APPENDIX B

CYBER-ATTACKS

How widespread are malicious attacks on computer systems? In answer to a Computer Security Institute poll, computer-security officials at 490 United States businesses, government agencies, financial institutions, medical institutions and universities reported the following types of attack or misuse over a twelve month period in 2003:

Virus	82%
Insider abuse of Internet access	80%
Laptop theft	59%
Unauthorized access by insiders	45%
Denial of service	42%
System penetration	36%
Theft of proprietary information	21%
Sabotage	21%
Financial fraud	15%
Telecom fraud	10%
Telecom eavesdropping	6%
Active wiretap	1%

The same survey listed the likely sources of attack as follows:

Web site incidents were of the following types:

Email attachment	86%
Internet downloads	11%
Web browsing	4%
Don't know	1%
Other	3%

Viruses came from the following sources:[4]

Disgruntled employees	86%
Independent hackers	74%
United States competitors	53%
Non-United States companies	30%
Governments	21%

[4] ICSA Labs. Figure note more than 100% due to multiple responses

And the monthly rate of infection per 1,000 PC's was as follows:5

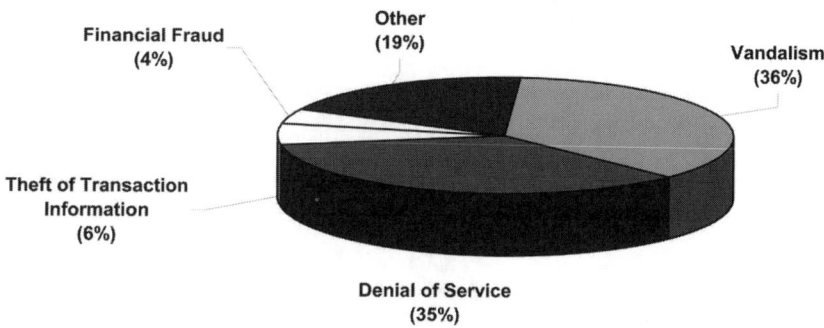

5 ICSA labs.

The financial impact, as reported by Computer Security Institute, was as follows:

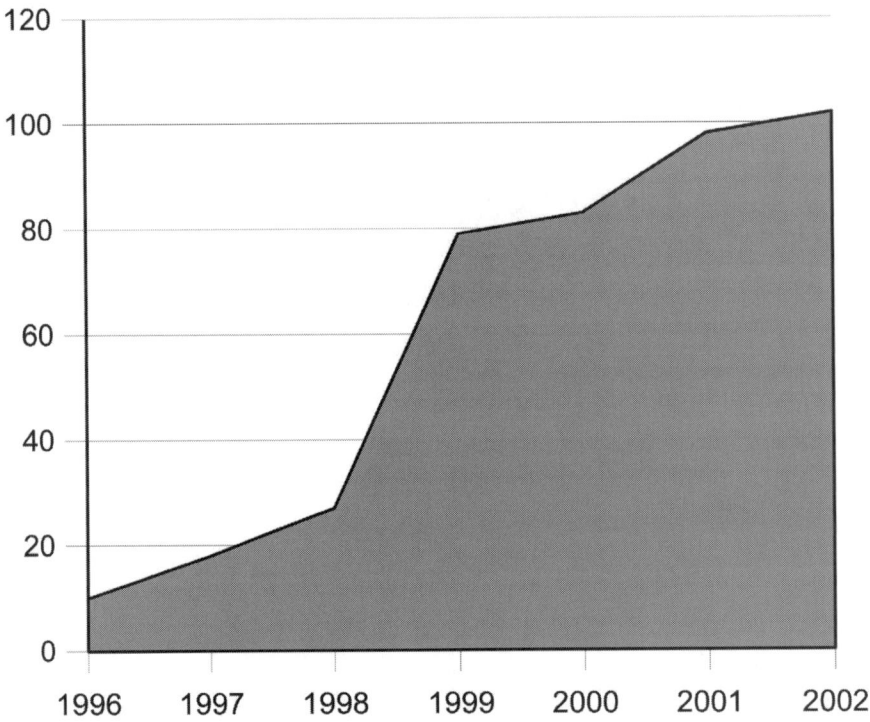

Theft of proprietary information	$70,195,900
Denial of service	65,643,300
Virus	27,382,340
Insider abuse of Internet access	11,767,200
Financial fraud	10,186,400
Laptop theft	6,830,500
Sabotage	5,148,500
System penetration	2,754,400
Active wiretap	705,000
Telecom fraud	701,500
Unauthorized access by insiders	406,300
Telecom eavesdropping	76,000

And companies spent the following on computer security software (in millions):[6]

Category	2002	2007	Growth[7]
Secure content management	2694.5	6379.5	18.8%
User authentication, authorization, administrative software	2487.3	5063.9	15.3%
Firewall/VPN software	891.7	1179.4	5.8%
Intrusion detection	723	548.51	6.4%
Encryption	249.2	518.2	15.8%

[6] Cumulative annual growth rate, 2002-07. Source: IDC.
[7] Includes antivirus, content filtering and antispam software

PART ONE

INTEGRATED SECURITY
A NEW WAY OF THINKING

CHAPTER ONE
NO KNOWLEDGE, NO SECURITY

Anonymous. "Fast and Present Danger: New Study Shows Majority of Broadband Users Lack 'Basic Online Protections.'" Retrieved Oct. 14, 2003, from http://www. staysafeonline.info.

Anonymous. "Overview: Security" (2002), pdf document. Cisco Systems, http://www. cisco.com.

Berinato, Scott. "The Homeland Brand." Oct. 26, 2003,from http://www2.cio.com/research/security/edit/a07312002.html.

Berinato, Scott. "No More Than the Obvious." Oct. 26, 2003, from http://www2.cio.com/research/security/edit/a09302003.html.

Berinato, Scott, "The Paranoia Paradox." Oct. 26, 2003, from http://www2.cio.com/research/security/edit/a08292002.html.

Boothe Ivan & Stossel Sage. "Flashbacks—Technology and Security," *The Atlantic Online*, August 21, 2002.
http://www.theatlantic.com/unbound/flashbks/techsecure.htm.

Budiansky, Stephen. "Losing the Code War," *The Atlantic Monthly*, February 2002.
http://www.theatlantic.com/issues/2002/02/budiansky.htm.

Carr, David. "The Futility of '"Homeland Defense,'"
The Atlantic Monthly, Boston: Jan 2002, Vol. 289, Iss. 1; pg. 53, 3 pgs. [electronic version,
http://www.theatlantic.com/issues/2002/01/carr.htm].

Christensen, John. "Bracing for Guerrilla Warfare in Cyberspace," April 6, 1999. http://www.cnn.com/TECH/specials/hackers/cyberterror.

Denning, Dorothy E. "Cyberterrorism: Testimony before the Special Oversight Panel on Terrorism Committee on Armed Services U.S. House of Representatives," Georgetown University, May 23, 2000. http://www.cs.georgetown.edu/~denning/ infosec/cyberterror.html.

Fallows, James. "Open Secrets," *The Atlantic Monthly*, September 2001.
http://www.theatlantic.com/issues/94jun/fallows.htm.

Kirn, Walter. "The Mother of Reinvention," *The Atlantic Monthly,* May 2002.
http://www.theatlantic.com/issues/2002/05/kirn.htm.

Murphy, Victoria. "Spook Valley," Dec. 10, 2001.
http://www.forbes.com/free_forbes/2001/1210/103.html.

Scalet, Sarah D. "The Latest Virus." Oct. 26, 2003,
http://www2.cio.com/research/security/edit/a05092002.html.

Scalet, Sarah D. "On Sept. 11." Oct. 26, 2003,
http://www2.cio.co.nz/cio.nsf/0/F33D18ECD87021C1CC256C7B000A5B3C

Scalet, Sarah D. "See Dick Resign." Oct. 26, 2003,
http://www2.cio.com/research/security/edit/a02032003.html.

CHAPTER TWO
PERSPECTIVES ON SECURITY

Anonymous, "Qualitative & Management Risk Analysis Techniques." Oct. 22, 2003, from http://www.gmtrust.com/riskanalysis.htm.

Anonymous, "What is cyberterrorism?," Council on Foreign Relations. Oct. 8, 2003,
http://www.terrorismanswers.com/terrorism/cyberterrorism.html.

Behar, Richard, "Business Goes to War: Fear along the Firewall," Fortune, October 1, 2001.
http://www.fortune.com/fortune/articles/ 0,15114,368010,00.html.
Behar, Richard "Who's Reading Your E-mail?," Fortune, February 3, 1997.
http://cba.fiu.edu/acg/floresj/acg6625/Articles/ Who'sReadingyourE-Mail.htm.

Berinato, Scott, "The First Internet Conflict? Why the Web Is Too Fast for War." Oct. 26, 2003,
http://ww.csoonline.com/alarmed/03312003.html.

Berinato, Scott, "The Security Spending Mystery." Oct. 26, 2003, from http://www.csoonline.com/alarmed/04252002.html.

Buderi, Robert, "The Virus Wars," *The Atlantic Monthly*, Boston: Apr 1999. Vol. 283, Iss. 4; pg. 32, 4 pgs [electronic version, http://www.theatlantic.com/issues/99apr/9904compuvirus.htm.]

Cole, Bernard, "Cyberterror, Embedded Systems, and the Second Shoe." Oct. 14, 2003,
http://www.embedded.com/story/OEG20020713S0001.

Dreazen, Yochi J., "The Sky is Falling?" *Wall Street Journal Europe* Friday/Saturday/Sunday October 3-5, 2003.

Dunham, Kemba J., "Escape Clause," *Wall Street Journal Europe* Friday/Saturday/Sunday October 3-5, 2003.

Hymowitz, Carol, and Totty, Michael, "How Vulnerable are You?" *Wall Street Journal Europe* Friday/Saturday/Sunday October 3-5, 2003.

Scalet, Sarah D., "Howard Schmidt Holds Court." Oct. 26, 2003, http://www.csoonline.com/alarmed/11122002.html.

Scalet, Sarah D., "Is Cybercrime Really Underreported?" Oct. 26, 2003, http://www2.cio.com/research/security/edit/a08152002.html.

Scalet, Sarah D., "Oh, Did We Forget to Mention That?" Oct. 26, 2003, http://www2.cio.com/research/security/edit/a03142003.html.

Scalet, Sarah D., "Rethinking Privacy." Oct. 26, 2003, http://www.csoonline.com/alarmed/09142001.html.

Scalet, Sarah D., "Risk Management." Oct. 26, 2003, http://www.csoonline.com/alarmed/07122001.html.

Scalet, Sarah D., "Taking Security to Market." Oct. 26, 2003, http://www2.cio.com/research/security/edit/a04112002.html.

Sesel, Jonathan, "Bridging Qualitative and Quantitative Analysis." Oct. 22, 2003, http://www.siliconrose.com.au/Articles/BridgingQualQuant.htm.

Thompson, Clive, "When Hackers Make House Calls," Fortune, October 9, 2000, http://www.business2.com/articles/mag/0,1640,8672,FF.html.

CHAPTER THREE
BUILDING SECURITY INTO THE CULTURE

Anonymous, "The convergence of viruses and spam: Lessons learned from the SoBig.F experience" (n.d.), pdf document, http://www.security.iia.net.au/downloads/sobigwhitepaper.pdf.

Anonymous, "Cyberterrorism Is Everyone's War," Oct. 11, 2001, http://www2.cio.com/research/security/edit/a10112001.html.

Anonymous, "Know Your Enemy - A Profile," June 6, 2003, pdf document, http://www.cisco.com.

Berinato, Scott, "Bad Guy Wisdom—Question: Who's more open and honest, hackers or corporate America?" Retrieved Oct. 26, 2003 http://www2.cio.com/research/security/edit/a06282001.html.

Berinato, Scott, "Conserve Privacy." Retrieved Oct. 26, 2003, http://www2.cio.com/research/security/edit/a12232002.html.

Berinato, Scott, "Guilty Until Proven Innocent: Smile, You're a Potential Shoplifter." Oct. 26, 2003, http://www2.cio.com/research/security/edit/a08062003.html.

Berinato, Scott, "Is the Sky Falling?." Oct. 26, 2003, http://www2.cio.com/research/security/edit/a10282002.html.

Berinato, Scott, "Only Mostly Dead—RIP PKI." Oct. 26, 2003, http://www2.cio.com/research/security/edit/a05232002.html.

Berinato, Scott, "Turn it Off, Turn it All Off." Oct. 26, 2003, http://www.csoonline.com/alarmed/09282001.html.

Boyd, Stowe, "Social Commentary: Cracking the Social Code." Oct. 26, 2003, http://www.darwinmag.com/read/090103/social.html.

Lidsky, David, "Computer Virus Insurance," Fortune, August 31, 2001.

Pollitt, Mark M., "Cyberterrorism - Fact or Fancy?" Oct. 8, 2003, http://www.cs.georgetown.edu/~denning/infosec/pollitt.html.

Quinlan, Heather, "Cyber Terrorism," October 14, 2003, http://www.tlc.discovery.com/convergence/hackers/ articles/cyberterror.html.

Richmond, Riva, "How to Find Your Weak Spots," *Wall Street Journal Europe* Friday/Saturday/Sunday October 3-5, 2003.

Scalet, Sarah D., "An Academic-Turned-Entrepreneur." Oct. 26, 2003, http://www2.cio.com/research/security/alarmed.html.

Scalet, Sarah D., "Chasing the Keystroke Capturers." Oct. 26, 2003, http://www2.cio.com/research/security/alarmed.html.

Scalet, Sarah D., "Security Guard for a Day." Oct. 26, 2003, http://www.csoonline.com/alarmed/09122002.html.

http://www.SecuriTeam.com

CHAPTER FOUR
KNOWLEDGE AND SECURITY

Anonymous, "Building In-Depth Security for Small and Midsize Business Networks," (2003), pdf document, http://www.cisco.com/warp/public/779/smbiz/ cibrchannel/documents/sec_wp.pdf.

Anonymous, "Palmer, Charles, Q&A with." Oct. 14, 2003, http://www-cgi.cnn.com/TECH/specials/ hackers/qandas/palmer.html.

http://www.attrition.org.

Berinato, Scott, "The Firewall Fetish." Oct. 26, 2003, http://www2.cio.com/research/security/edit/a07262001.html.

Berinato, Scott, "Missed Opportunity." Oct. 26, 2003, http://www.csoonline.com/alarmed/03282002.html.

Berinato, Scott, "Still Hardly Trustworthy?" Oct. 26, 2003, http://www2.cio.com/research/security/edit/a02272003.html.

Berinato, Scott, "Strategy*—How a year's worth of work was undermined by an asterisk." Oct. 26, 2003,
http://www2.cio.com/research/security/alarmed.html.

Gillen, Nicole, "Techs and the City." Oct. 28, 2003,
http://www.lightreading.com/document.asp?doc_id=35288.

Green, Joshua, "The Myth of Cyberterrorism," *The Washington Monthly*, November 2002,
http://www.washingtonmonthly.com/features/ 2001/0211.green.html.

Hamilton, David P., "Read My Lips," *Wall Street Journal Europe* Friday/Saturday/Sunday October 3-5, 2003.

Hundt, Reed, "Keeping the Net Secure," *The Atlantic Monthly,* Boston: Jan 2002. Vol. 289, Iss. 1; pg. 26, 2 pgs. [electronic edition, http://www.theatlantic.com/issues/2002/01/hundt.htm.]

Kirkpatrick, David, "Fast Forward: Securing Cyberspace," Fortune, September 10, 2002,
http://www.cnn.com.

Mandeville, David, "Hackers, Crackers and Trojan Horses: a Primer," March 29, 1999,
http://www.cnn.com/TECH/specials/hackers/primer.

Powell, Brad, "Lessons from Honeynet." Oct. 13, 2003,
http://honeynet.org.

Scalet, Sarah D., "On the Offense." Oct. 26, 2003,
http://www2.cio.com/research/security/edit/a04242003.html.

Scalet, Sarah D., "Spoofed!," Jan. 16, 2003,
http://www.csoonline.com/alarmed/01162003.html.

Sloane, Julie, "PC Viruses—Latest Terrorism?" Fortune, September 28, 2001.

Spitzner, Lance, "They Gain Root, Know Your Enemy: III. Oct. 14, 2003, http://www.project.honeynet.org/papers/enemy3.

Totty, Michael, "Business Solutions," *Wall Street Journal Europe* Friday/Saturday/Sunday October 3-5, 2003.

PART TWO
KNOWLEDGE SYSTEMS AND SECURING BUSINESS INTELLIGENCE

CHAPTER FIVE
KNOWLEDGE AS AN ASSET

Anonymous, "Knowledge Management Critical for Start-ups." Oct. 28, 2003, http://www.realkm.blog-city.com/read/31857.htm.

Beazley, Hamilton, Ph.D., "Knowledge Continuity: The New Competitive Advantage." Oct. 8, 2003, http://www.centeronline.org/programs/ program.cfm?ProgramID=1180.

Beazley, Hamilton, Ph.D., "Knowledge Continuity in the Information Age" (n.d.) pdf document, http://www.centeronline.org/knowledge/article.cfm?ID=2314.

Berinato, Scott, "Marketing Forces." Oct. 26, 2003, http://www2.cio.com/research/security/edit/a09222003.html.

Chabot, Hillary, "Laid-off Jakes, Cops Hired Back," BY/ Journal Staff, Thursday, August 28, 2003, http://www.townonline.com/somerville/news/local_regional/ sj_covsjretirems08282003.htm.

Drucker, Peter, "When Knowledge Walks…" Oct. 28, 2003, http://www.intraxltd.com/reports/FactSheets/ ProcedureNetOverview.doc.

Kirsner, Scott, "Why is It That…?" Oct. 26, 2003,
http://www.darwinmag.com/read/030102/ecosystem.html.

Lester, Toby, "The Reinvention of Privacy," *The Atlantic Monthly*, Boston: Mar 2001. Vol. 287, Iss. 3; pg. 27, 13 pgs. [electronic version, http://www.theatlantic.com/issues/2001/03/lester-p1.htm.]

Santosus, Megan, "KM Works Magic for Ketchum," August 17, 2001,
http://www.cio.com/research/knowledge/edit/ketchum.html.

Santosus, Megan, "Northrop Grumman,." Oct. 26, 2003,
http://www.cio.com/archive/090101/thanks.html.

Surmacz, Jon, "What Is Knowledge Management?" Oct. 26, 2003,
http://www.cio.com/research/knowledge/edit/kmabcs.html.

Weber, Beth, "Xerox Endows Distinguished Professorship in Knowledge." Oct. 28, 2003,
http://www.haas.berkeley.edu/calbusiness/ f97articles/f97.8.html.

Weinstein, Bob, "Prevent High Staff Turnover With These Tactics." Oct. 28, 2003,
http://www.techrepublic.com.com/5102-6297-1048252.html.

CHAPTER SIX
DYNAMICS OF KM: KNOWLEDGE JUNCTIONS

EVOLVENT Technologies
"Knowledge Junction is a registered trademark of EVOVENT"

Anonymous, "Managing Unstructured Content in Enterprise Information Portals," July 16, 2001, Unitas Corp.
http://www.destinationkm.com/articles/ default.asp?ArticleID=322.

Boyd, Stowe, "Social Commentary: Swarm Intelligence," July 01, 2003,
http://www.darwinmag.com/read/070103/swarm.html.

Campbell, Sheila, "Creating a Knowledge Management System." Oct. 28, 2003,
http://www.business-marketing.com/store/abknowledge.html.

Compton, Jason, "British Telecommunications." Oct. 26, 2003,
http://www.cio.com/archive/061501/dial_content.html.

Dawson, Ross, "Innovation: Making Distributed Innovation Work," excerpt from Living Networks: Leading Your Company, Customers, and Partners in the Hyper-Connected Economy. Oct. 26, 2003,
http://www.livingnetworksbook.com

Mitchell, Meg, "Knowledge Management." Oct. 26, 2003,
http://www.darwinmag.com/read/020101/share.html.

O'Dell, Carla Ph.D., "Knowledge Management: What's Now and What's Next" Oct. 26, 2003,
http://www.chips.navy.mil/archives/02_winter/index2_files/knowledge_management.htm.

Ross, Ronald, "Principles of the Business Rule Approach." Oct. 26, 2003,
http://www.informit.com.

CHAPTER SEVEN
OPTIMAL ACCESSIBILITY

Anonymous, "Challenges Currently Faced with Learning Objects." Oct. 26, 2003,
http://www.learnware.uwaterloo.ca/projects/ CCCO/cloe

Barclay, Rebecca O., "The CKO — vision, strategy, ambassadorial skills, and a certain je ne sais quoi," KM Briefs and KM Metazine. Oct. 26, 2003,
http://www.ktic.com/topic6/13_CKO.HTM.

Bresnahan, Mary, "Cross Training for Success," reprinted from Springs magazine, February 2003,
http://www.bresnahangroup.com/articles/crosstraining.htm.

Chapman, Rod, "Helping the Group to Think Straight," Information Highways, May/June 2003,
http://www.darwinmag.com/read/080103/group.html.

Holtshouse, Dan, "Knowledge Domains–Model of a Knowledge-Driven Company?" Oct. 28, 2003,
http://www.crmproject.com/authors.asp?a_id=302.

Shein Esther, "Frito-lay's Sales Force." Oct. 26, 2003,
http://www.cio.com/archive/050101/crunch.html.

CHAPTER EIGHT
PROTECTING THE HUMAN CAPITAL

EVOLVENT White Paper–Knowledge Junctions,
www.evolvent.com

Anonymous, "All-time Low Employee Tenure Draining Knowledge out of Companies, Survey Shows." Oct. 28, 2003,
http://www.teradata.com.

Anonymous, "Competitor Evaluation and Action Plans."
Oct. 28, 2003,
http://www.winsightsolutions.com

Anonymous, "Latest News, Brain Drain hits IT companies." Oct. 28, 2003,
http://www.bizjournals.com/sanjose/stories/
2002/04/29/daily72.html bizjournal.com.

Kay, Alan S., "Harvest Your Knowledge to Boost Competitive Advantage," January 1, 2002,
http://www.basex.com/press.nsf/0/
E5EB74F7D3B32D4385256C8F0005F405?OpenDocument.

Lublin, Joann S., "No Place Like Home," *Wall Street Journal Europe* Friday/Saturday/Sunday October 3-5, 2003

Santosus, Megan, "Insurance giant CNA." Oct. 26, 2003, http://www.cio.com/research/knowledge/case.html.

PART THREE
CASE STUDIES

CHAPTER NINE
LEADERS IN KNOWLEDGE MANAGMENT

Anonymous, "Performance Appraisals Made Easy." Oct. 28, 2003, from http://www.njmep.org.

http://www.knowledgepoint.com.au/knowledge_management/Articles/KM_MP001a.htm

http://www.worldbank.org/ks.

CHAPTER TEN
CYBER-SECURITY INITIATIVES IN THE FEDERAL SECTOR

Harris, Master Sgt. Michael, "Usafe NOSC Knows How to Provide Network Security." Oct. 28, 2003, http://www.public.afca.af.mil.

The CERT® Coordination Center FAQ, http://www.cert.org.

CHAPTER ELEVEN
UNDERSTANDING THE COST DRIVERS

EVOLVENT's Case Studies

PART FOUR
LESSONS LEARNED

CHAPTER TWELVE
GLOBAL ALERT NETWORK

Berinato, Scott, "The Hunting of the Snark." Oct. 26, 2003, http://www2.cio.com/research/security/edit/a05212003.html.

Mann, Charles C., "Homeland Insecurity," *The Atlantic Monthly;* September 2002; Volume 290, No. 2; pp 81–102. [electronic version, http://www.theatlantic.com/issues/2002/09/mann.htm.]

Scalet, Sarah D., "Without Warning."Oct. 26, 2003, http://www2.cio.com/research/security/edit/a10102002.html.

AFTERWORD

APPENDIX A
HACKERS

Anonymous, "Goldstein, Emmanuel, Q&A with." Oct. 28, 2003, http://www.cnn.com/TECH/specials/hackers/ qandas/goldstein.html.

Anonymous, "Know Your Enemy: Motives—The Motives and Psychology of the Black-Hat Community," Honeynet Project, 27 June, 2000, http://www.project.honeynet.org/papers/motives.

Anonymous, "Know Your Enemy: The Tools and Methodologies of the Script Kiddie." Retrieved Oct. 13, 2003, from Honeynet Project, http://www.project.honeynet.org/papers/enemy.

http://www.ccpower.com.

Quittner, Jeremy, "Hacker Psych 101." Oct. 14, 2003, http://www.tlc.discovery.com/convergence/ hackers/articles/psych.html.

Quittner, Jeremy, "Hackers: Methods of Attack and Defense."Oct. 14, 2003, http://www.tlc.discovery.com/convergence/ hackers/articles/method.html.

Raymond, Eric S. "The Lingo of Hackerdom," adapted from The New Hacker's Dictionary (MIT Press, 2003). [electronic version, http://www.tlc.discovery.com/convergence/hackers/ glossary/glossary.html.]

Walton, Andy, "Scenes from a Mall: Friday Night by the Cinnabon with the 'Hacker Underground'," March 29, 1999, http://www.cnn.com/TECH/specials/hackers/culture.

APPENDIX B
STATISTICS

Wall Street Journal Europe
Friday/Saturday/Sunday October 3-5, 2003.

In addition, the following three sources were used in a variety of sections of this book:

Mitnick Kevin D. and Simon William L., *The Art of Deception*, Wiley Publishing Inc., Indianapolis, Indiana, 2002.

Schneier, Bruce, *Beyond Fear: Thinking Sensibly about Security in an Uncertain World*, Copernicus Books New York, NY, 2003.

Schneier, Bruce, *Secrets and Lies: Digital Security in a Networked World*, John Wiley and Sons, Inc., New York, NY 2000.

Robert Pinto

Bob Pinto is EVOLVENT's Vice-President for Knowledge Management. Prior to joining EVOVLENT, Mr. Pinto was Executive Project Manager and Principal in National KM Practice at IBM Corporation and previous similar roles at EDS Corporation and PRC Corporation. As a Senior Program Manager, he combines his extensive experience as a Knowledge Management/Organizational Learning practitioner with the ability to sell, design, implement and manage enterprise Knowledge Management and Learning projects. He has lead consulting engagements and intellectual capital related projects for federal government agencies and Fortune 500 companies. His skills have been applied to all aspects of the project life cycle from initial consultation though deployment and operations. Bob has demonstrated outstanding interpersonal skills in building successful business relationships and is a strong multi-disciplinary team leader. Bob holds a Masters Degree from George Washington University in Computer Science and a Bachelor of Science Degree in Mathematics from the University of Texas at Austin.

Paul Ramsaroop

Chief Technology Officer and EVOLVENT's Senior Vice President of Operations has served previously as CIO, Infonomic Solutions; CTO, HealthCPR Technologies; Program Manager, IntelliDyne, LLC; and Knowledge Manager, Maryville Technologies. In addition, Paul has over seven years of computer engineering experience at Boeing Corporation and McDonnell-Douglas Corporation. Paul attended University of Missouri, majoring in mathematics and computer science.

Guy Sherburne

Senior Director, Federal Cyber Security Services and Division Chief–San Antonio Operations, Mr. Sherburne is responsible for the development, implementation, and maintenance of DOD security service contracts. He previously served as Senior Systems Security Engineer at PEC Solutions, Inc and as Senior Systems Analyst at Troy Systems, Inc. Before that, Mr. Sherburne served 26 years in the U.S.Air Force. His USAF career included Chief Inspector for the NSA Inspector General and Chief Inspector for the Air Intelligence Agency Inspector General. His accomplishments encompass CENTCOM Special Security officer for Operation Southern Watch, the evacuation of South Vietnam, NASA's APOLLO post-launch debriefing and was named Strategic Air Command Information Security Program Manager of the Year. Mr. Sherburne has certifications in Information Assurance Management, SCI Security Management, and Force Protection Management. Mr. Sherburne currently holds a Top Secret Clearance.

Dennis R. Buxton

Senior Director of Cyber Consulting Services for EVOLVENT, including assignments as program director, Network Operations and Security Center (NOSC) for the U.S. Army Medical Command; He previously served as an Information Warfare Flight (IWF) Program Manager for the U.S. Air Force's Air Intelligence Agency, overseeing the programmatic infrastructure and deployment of IW assets worldwide. Dennis received his dual bachelors degrees in Communications and Management/Computer Information Systems from the University of Missouri and Park University, respectively. He has been certified by the SANS Institute as an Information Security Officer (GISO). Dennis has also served as a critical member and trainer conducting computer network defense operations for the USAF and helped developed the CONOPS for the USAF-level NOSC. He holds a Top Secret Clearance.

Other Books from EVOLVENT Press

Surfing the Leadership Wave by Peter R. Ramsaroop, 2003. 209+xiv pp. $24.95

Detailed Information on these and all other EVOLVENT titles may be found at www.evolventpress.com or by calling 1-703-379-2146.

INDEX

attacks, 11-17, 27, 28, 32, 36, 37, 58, 66, 72, 73, 85, 99, 156-159, 176, 178-180, 190, 197, 199
    access, 11, 12, 21, 59, 61, 63, 65, 66, 72-76, 178, 197, 199
    corrupted mobile code, 67
    cross site scripting, 67
    data interception, 67
    denial of service 13, 14, 65-67, 84, 87, 157, 197, 203
    email spoofing, 67
    physical theft, 67
    reconnaissance, 66
    scams, 67
backdoor, 21, 70, 193, 197
    program, 72, 191-194, 196
best practice implementation, 166, 170
business intelligence, 15, 89, 149, 163-165, 189, 212

BW/CW, 181
CCPower, 192, 193, 217
Centers for Disease Control, CDC, 179, 180
centers of excellence, 111, 112
CERT, 86, 154-156, 158, 216
certification, 161
collaboration areas, 113, 114
    asynchronous communication, 114, 122, 148
    COTS applications, 122
    synchronous communication, 114, 122
content channels, 147
content management, 117, 118, 121, 123, 127, 140, 144, 145, 151
    document conversion, 121
    document management, 117, 121
    records management, 121
contingency planning (COP), 36, 51, 125, 126, 128
controls, 28, 29, 32, 34, 35
    authorization, 25

corrective, 14, 32
detective, 32
deterrent, 32
network, 25, 29, 34, 35, 38, 39
preventative, 32
corporate culture, 99
critical design review, 80
cryptography, 19
culture of security, 56-58, 62, 87
customer service best practices, 165
cyber dangers, 16
impact, 16
national boundaries, 16
technical resources, 16
cyber-crime, 1, 65
cyber-criminals, 11, 69
cyber-revolution, 132
cyber-security, 1, 24, 27, 28, 61, 84, 91, 153, 216
environmental threats, 24
internal attacks, 15
external attacks, 15
natural threats, 23, 24, 25, 178
cyber-terrorism, 11, 12, 16, 25, 160
cyber-threats, 11, 17, 28, 154
data management, 165, 166
denial of service, 13, 14, 65, 66, 67, 73, 84, 87, 157, 197
department of homeland security, 7, 175-177, 179, 180, 184
distance learning, 98, 123, 127, 140

document repository, 113, 117, 144, 145
encryption, 3, 61, 75-78, 132, 182, 204
email, 2, 8, 9, 13, 24, 30-32, 45, 56, 58, 59, 61, 66, 67, 69, 70, 72, 76, 87, 99, 101, 102, 106, 114, 115, 120, 122, 146-148
Ethernet, 21, 197
evident surprise, 157
EVOLVENT, 109, 144, 154, 160, 163, 164, 213, 215, 222, 223
expertise, 2, 39-41, 86, 110, 111, 113, 116, 117, 122, 139, 147, 148, 151, 160, 164, 168, 176
affinity groups, 122, 125, 150
association, 19, 21, 122, 147
directories, 35, 112, 122, 147
mining, 122, 147
explicit knowledge, 2, 170
FEMA, 176, 180
file integrity checkers, 38
firewalls, 3, 9, 11, 25, 43, 68, 75, 120, 147
GAN TV, 182
Global Alert Network (GAN), 3, 175-186, 216
Global Development Learning Network (GDLN), 139, 140

hackers, 11, 13, 17, 19, 25, 28, 40, 41, 73-75, 83, 119, 153, 159, 161, 190, 192, 194, 196-198, 200, 206, 208-211, 217, 218
hierarchical site map, 111-113
human capital domain, 2, 3, 120, 129
    communities of practice, 124-126, 128, 139, 149, 150
    enterprise strategy, 151
    governance, 127, 149
    marketing, 101, 102, 127, 149, 150, 165, 169, 213
    organizational learning, 148, 151, 219
    performance measures, 126, 127, 150
    rewards, 103, 126, 151
    trust systems, 128, 150
human issues, 124
    populate COP, 125
    team rooms, 98, 122, 125, 148
IA architecture, 156
IA limitations, 155
implementation model, 144, 145, 150
index of concepts, 113
institutional awareness, 123, 147
Internet, 1, 8, 9, 11, 13, 14, 18, 20, 21, 26, 48, 58, 60, 65, 66, 68, 69, 71-75, 81, 82, 84, 85, 87, 88, 91, 106, 113, 116, 133, 134, 153, 154, 157, 160, 161, 180, 190, 192-194, 196, 198, 199, 203, 207

intranet, 21, 101, 106, 109, 111, 113, 117, 118, 120, 144, 152
intrusion detection system (I.D.S.), 86
IPV4, 81-83
IPV6, 81-84
IT budgeting, 171, 172
IT security, 170
JTF-CND, 156, 158, 159
knowledge security, 3, 10, 108
knowledge protection, 15
knowledge assets, 108
knowledge center, 143
knowledge junction, 100, 109-118, 120, 138, 144, 145, 152, 175
knowledge management, 2, 3, 7, 92, 93, 97-100, 102-107, 109, 120, 129, 133, 137-142, 164, 175, 181, 185, 188, 213, 219
knowledge sharing, 116, 137-139, 144, 145, 151, 164, 165, 170
KX, 145-151
learning management system, 113, 118
misappropriation of knowledge, 132
Netbus, 194
network mapping, 38
nominal software, 23
NOSC, 154-156, 161, 162, 216, 222
optimal access, 119, 120
peer reviewer, 116

personal security, 35, 56, 87, 97
physical threats, 11
pilot program, 80
pointer file, 113
preliminary design review, 80
proprietary knowledge, 10, 47
public key infrastructure, 77
    authentication, 75, 77
    confidentiality, 77, 78, 84
ranking system, 107
Remedy, 25, 168
risk assessment, 26, 28-30, 43, 45, 154
risk management, 32, 45, 46, 48, 164, 166
    business risk, 49, 50
    organizational risk, 49, 50
    security risk, 16, 29, 49
    technical risk, 49
ROI, 156, 170
script kiddies, 11, 153, 198
search & navigation
    content clustering, 121, 146
    taxonomy, 23, 113, 117, 121, 122, 146, 147
    thematic searches, 121, 146
    thesaurus, 121, 146
    web crawlers, 121, 146
security configuration management, 36
security awareness training, 84
security features, 11, 36, 83, 117
security practices, 7, 16, 60, 188
security tools, 68
    anti-spyware software, 68
    anti-virus software, 68
    email attachments, 32, 69, 72
    file sharing, 69, 72, 73
    passwords, 11, 12, 35, 36, 43, 68, 74, 120, 146, 157, 188, 193
security patches, 25, 69, 71, 83, 159, 167
security training, 35, 159
service desk technologies, 168, 169
social engineer, 13, 59-61
software holes, 19
spidering, 115
Stellent, 145
strategic compact, 138
Surfing the Leadership Wave, 98, 223
tacit knowledge, 2, 12, 91, 92, 100, 103, 106, 111, 113, 114, 139
technical infrastructure, 120, 146
    reliable 24/7 operations, 120
    telecommunications, 120, 147, 159, 178, 184, 213
    universal directory, 120, 146
technological domain, 120
technology domain, 2, 3, 120, 129
telephony systems, 169
testing, 38-41, 81, 83, 155
    dialing attack, 38, 42
    log review, 38
    password cracking, 38, 40
    penetration, 38, 155

security/evaluation, 38
vulnerability, 37-39, 91, 154, 155
threats, 11, 17, 21-24, 26, 28, 29, 33, 37, 43, 44, 46, 49, 59, 60, 66, 81, 82, 84, 94, 119, 154-156, 160, 175, 176, 178, 179, 182, 183, 185, 188, 198
    biological, 179, 181-184
    chemical, 179, 182-184
    nuclear, 183, 184
Total Cost of Ownership (TCO) assessment, 163-165, 171, 172
Trojan horses, 11, 25, 211
unstructured knowledge, 101
    discussion threads, 102
    groupware applications, 101
    intranet sites, 101
    multi-media files, 102
    public websites, 101
    word processing, 101, 102
user profiling, 123
    user interface, 123
    personalization, 123
    user profiling, 123
VA-CIRC, 160, 161
VAST, 92, 108, 109, 117, 160, 185
Vignette, 140
virus, 3, 9, 13, 20, 31, 32, 38, 42, 48, 66, 68-72, 99, 100, 155, 197-199, 203, 206, 207, 209

detectors, 38
scanner, 20, 38, 39
scans, 9, 39, 82, 86
vulnerabilities, 1, 11, 24, 26, 28, 32-34, 38-41, 44, 48, 51, 60, 71, 84, 155-157, 160, 178, 198
    application level software, 36
    environmental systems, 37
    facilities, 49, 57, 75, 140, 142, 179, 182, 186
    historical data, 36
    operational data, 84
    personal, 9, 14, 19, 21, 24, 25, 35, 48, 56, 67, 78, 83, 84, 87, 94, 97-100, 106, 108, 114, 130, 133, 153, 160, 191, 194, 197
vulnerability assessment, 26, 28, 29, 37, 38
    annual loss expectancy, 30
    cyber-theft, 26
    estimated annual cost, 30
    qualitative risk analysis, 30, 32
    quantitative risk analysis, 30
web availability, 138
workflow, 122, 125
    departmental business processes, 123
    web content management approval, 123
World Bank, 137, 138, 140
worms, 11, 25, 82, 119, 153